Teaching English

for

Medical Purposes

by Virginia Allum

ISBN 978-1-291-07412-3

90000

Contents

Virginia Allum

co-author of two 'Cambridge English for Nursing' books and author of several 'English for Medical Purposes' books (for doctors, nurses and nursing assistants). She is a practising Registered Nurse with current experience in the UK and previous experience in Australia. She is a consultant in English for Medical Purposes with a particular focus on English for Nursing, writes a regular blog on her website www.e4nursingandhealthcare.com/ and is a guest contributor to infermiers.com, French online nursing magazine. Virginia recently co-presented at the first UK Teacher Training in EMP seminar and develops course materials and resources in EMP and EMP teacher training. She lives in the South-West of England.

   **EMP articles on**

http://www.authorsden.com/virginiajallum

Webpage :

www.englishfornursingandhealthcare.com

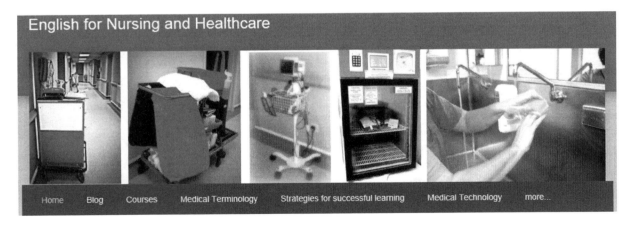

Business Spotlight

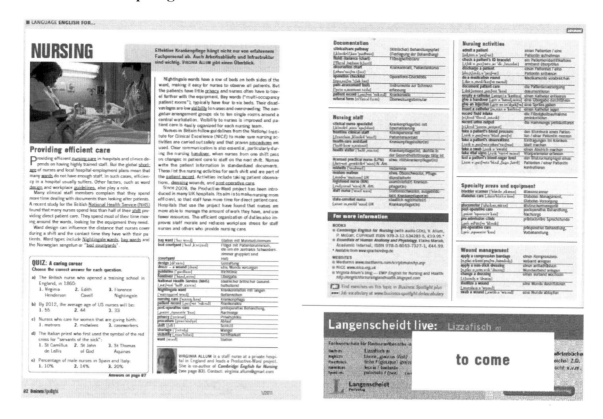

Infermiers.com

Facebook : English for Nursing and Healthcare

Cambridge Press : free teacher resources

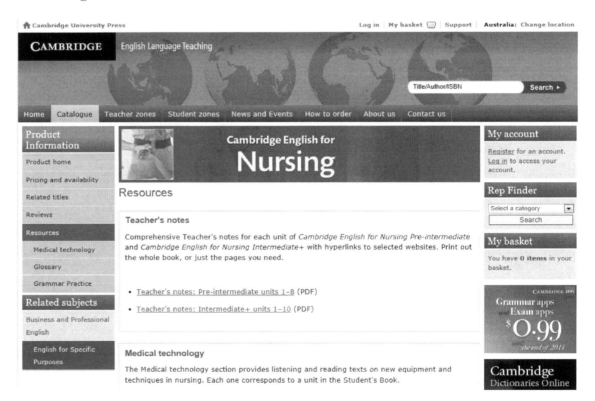

Term	Meaning
ESP	English for Specific Purposes
LSP	Language for Specific Purposes
EMP	English for Medical Purposes
PAL	Pre-Arrival Learning
CNA	Certified Nursing Assistant
HCA	Health Care Assistant
RN	Registered Nurse
RM	Registered Midwife
EN	Enrolled Nurse
EEN	Endorsed Enrolled Nurse
HCP	Health Care Professional

Day 1
Session 1: Teaching English for Healthcare Professionals as a Non-practitioner

Many ELT trainers 'fear' or at best are wary of the Medical English classroom and its occupants: concerns about inadequate knowledge of medicine, grappling with terminology and generally feeling 'unsure' of their role and the benefits such a collaboration might bring. The presenter will give an overview of teaching medical communications in English and hopefully debunk a few of the myths linked to training professionals from the field of medicine.

Session 2: Areas in Healthcare: An Overview

This session introduces the main areas of Healthcare practice for the multi-disciplinary team. Among the subjects discussed will be the discourse and register used in a variety of practice areas, including Paediatrics, Gerontology and Accident and Emergency. Also to be considered will be the Code of Practice and Code of Ethics for Healthcare Professionals and the possible linguistic implications for our learners.

Session 3: Evaluation of Published Materials for Teaching EMP

Compare notes on collecting and collating resources currently at the disposal of EMP trainers. This session seeks to identify and evaluate materials currently available to the trainer (course books as well as online) and other available resources and explores the challenges in their effective management. Input from course participants and teacher trainer alike promises an informative and practical workshop.

Session 4: Developing Activities for Medical English Vocabulary

In this session we will consider the vocabulary needs of our students, take a fresh look at 'semi-technical' vocabulary, discuss strategies for handling more specialised lexis and assess the use of word lists derived from authentic corpora. We will also look at some techniques for teaching and developing the vocabulary of medical English learners.

What is English for Medical Purposes?

from http://www.squidoo.com/emp-english-for-medical-purposes

English for Medical Purposes is one of the areas of ESP or English for Specific Purposes. Recently it has become clear that specialised knowledge in healthcare terms and competence in communication in the healthcare environment is a vital part of providing patients with safe care. Hospitals are often difficult places to work in because of the pressured environment. This can be difficult for healthcare workers who may have to communicate with patients and colleagues under stressful conditions. All the more reason to have a solid background in the language needed to work in an English-speaking healthcare environment.

It is always important to do a needs analysis before starting any new course, especially in areas of specialisation such as Medical English. An assessment of students' level of General English and any knowledge of the specialised area about to be taught is vital so that the course you teach will be relevant to student needs and be delivered at a level which is manageable for students. It will also give teachers an idea of areas of interests which students may have. This is important to know if there are discussion points you want to have during the course. Students who are interested in a topic or want to know about a topic are more likely to contribute to discussions

What is English for Medical Purposes?

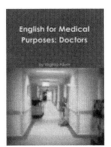

English for Medical Purposes is a type of ESP or English for Specific Purposes. There are a number of specialised areas in ESP which have grown up in response to the needs of the workplace. Courses such as English for Business Purposes, Law, Finance, Aviation, Oil and Gas, Marketing ...and the list goes on. Specialised courses were developed when it became clear that students who had completed English language courses at Advanced level were still not able to manage the kind of language they would encounter when they start work in an English-speaking environment. An English-speaking environment may be in an English-speaking country such as the UK or the USA or it may be the student's own country where English is the common language of communication.

EMP, Aviation English and Oil and Gas English have similar additional requirements i.e the need to develop communication skills which ensure safety in the workplace. This can have an effect on course structure - it's important to make sure that role plays are authentic or near-authentic and give enough practice in the sort of scenarios which may cause concern in the workplace. At the same time, there is a lot of technical language to learn and use in context. EMP courses have to be a balance between serious communication examples and a bit of fun!

Where is EMP used?

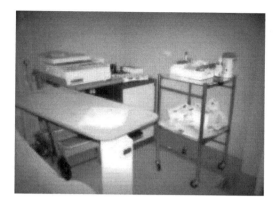

English for Medical Purposes encompasses many areas of need and is growing all the time. Students of EMP may have one or more of the following needs :

1. A workplace orientated course e.g overseas doctors and nurses who come to work in the UK. There is an increasing need for proof of language competency in healthcare workers before they are able to start work in an English-speaking healthcare environment. Language testing of all overseas-trained doctors and nurses is currently on the agenda in the UK - at present only non-EU doctors and nurses have their language skills tested. This sometimes has the absurd result that healthcare workers from countries such as Australia, New Zealand and South Africa have to sit a language test before being able to register in the UK but healthcare workers from Europe do not.

2. A workplace orientated course for doctors and nurses who care for English-speaking patients in their own country. Many healthcare consumers are travelling all over the world to access cheaper healthcare e.g cosmetic surgery. English is often the common language between patient and healthcare worker. People also travel widely for holidays and to attend global sporting events such as The Olympics or The World Cup. Healthcare workers are

called on to communicate with overseas visitors who fall ill or are injured in a language common to both - usually English.

3. PAL (Pre-Arrival Learning) or training in the language needed for university courses. This may be undertaken online or as a pre-sessional course. PAL courses are becoming more and more popular as students try to be as prepared as possible for courses they undertake overseas. These days students make considerable financial commitments to be able to study abroad. They cannot afford to spend time honing English language skills after arrival. By studying a PAL course, students have a better chance of understanding content when they start their degree or diploma.

4. a compulsory part of an overseas medical or nursing curriculum e.g the French Nursing Diploma has a compulsory EMP sector. French nursing students prepare during their course for their final semester assessment of a critique of an academic article in English.

5. an online course to improve language competency. Online courses may form part of Blended Learning during a f2f course or stand alone. Some students like to continue to improve their EMP skills even after starting work. This often gives them the chance to practise areas which they feel less sure of.

What specialised language is taught in an EMP class?

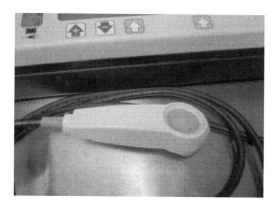

EMP teaches the language used to talk about healthcare. It is a mix of medical terminology and everyday health terms which are needed to communicate with patients. There are also vocabulary needs e.g the names of medical equipment, procedures and tests.

An EMP course which focuses on communication in the workplace rather than academic communication will cover the communication focus between the healthcare worker and patients, colleagues, other HCPs (Health Care Professional). This will include language found in General English courses but which is used in a healthcare context ,e.g

- Asking for information (on admission)

- Giving instructions (medication use, wound care)

- Asking about past habits (ask about past medical history)

- Talking about pain level (location, intensity)

- Passing on information e.g in handovers. Handovers (also called Handoffs) are exchanges of information between heath care workers to provide information about patient care and changed patient care status. This may be done between shifts; the outgoing shift will hand over information to the oncoming shift. They may pass on messages e.g test times and remind staff about future activities e.g discharge planning information. Handovers may also be used informally to pass on patient information e.g after medical review, return from a test.

- Talking on the phone. This may involve talking messages or phoning other departments to ask for or give information about a patient, to make a referral or to make an appointment. Incoming calls from patients' friends and relations can be quite difficult as Data Protection laws prevent staff from passing on any information to unauthorised people.

- Calling for medical assistance, sometimes by phone using the SBAR technique (gathering information about the patient under the headings of Situation, Background, Assessment, Recommendation)

- Talking about procedures e.g checking drugs or explaining the steps of a procedure (what is going to happen) to a patient

- Asking about feelings - this is important in the area of pain management and Palliative Care and is quite difficult to manage.

Other EMP specific areas need to be covered as well, for example

Appropriate writing focus (hospital documents, charts, patient record)

Medical terminology and everyday health terminology

Appropriate reading focus (care pathways, drug info, policies and procedures)

What is LSP?

LSP or Language for Specific Purposes is an area of applied linguistics which is used in the teaching of specialised needs in any foreign language. The language which is focused on usually relates to a need for a job or study. Another use of the language is to research variations of language within a particular subject.

LSP in English is described as English for Specific Purposes or ESP. An example of the use of LSP is the common situation for doctors and nurses in the USA who find themselves needing to communicate with Spanish-speaking patients with poor Health Literacy, that is little knowledge of Medical English terms relating to their own health. In this case, the LSP is Spanish for Medical Purposes.

The second arm of LSP is the use in linguistic research. This is used in training for interpreting and translation and writing technical or specialised dictionaries, for example medical dictionaries. Medical dictionaries contain medical terms and also health-related or hospital-related terms. Some terms have an everyday equivalent which may have a different or slightly different meaning.

For example, in Medical English

'discharge' means either 'the secretions which ooze out of a wound' or 'patients leaving the hospital for home or transfer to another health facility'.

'observations' mean 'vital signs and an overview of a patient's general status'

These are two words which have different meanings in a general sense.

LSP is contrasted with CBI or Content-based language instruction. Previously, CBI used to refer to the 'grammar-translation' method of teaching a foreign language which many of us (if you are over 40!) will be familiar with. The 'content', that is list of vocabulary words was presented at the beginning of the unit and followed by a translation passage which was probably written in an awkward style because it attempted to include as many examples of the grammar point of the particular unit. This resulted in many students saying that they had studied French for four years but were unable to make themselves understood when they actually landed in France and tried to order a meal!

These days, the term 'content' refers to the use of subject matter as a vehicle for second or foreign language learning. An example of this is the following Lesson Plan

Where Food Comes From

Students choose their favourite fruit and vegetable and classify whether it grows in cold or

hot countries. Students classify vegetables as 'eaten cooked', 'eaten raw' and 'all of it is eaten'.

Students can also classify fruit and vegetables as 'growing on trees', 'growing on bushes' or

'growing in the ground'.

Activities include: Apple Poem. Fruit quiz.

LANGUAGE: Names of fruit and vegetables, colours, sentence patterns 'Tomatoes are red;

tomatoes grow on bushes.'

THINKING: Classifying types of food.

CBI teaching was officially sanctioned by the European Commission in 1995 when it was

renamed CLIL or Content and Language Integrated Learning because it is language teaching

which is integrated into the L1 or first language curriculum

What is PAL?

PAL stands for Pre-Arrival Learning. Pre-Arrival Learning is something which most Colleges or Universities agree is extremely useful, however, few seem to offer. I used to teach in a Diploma of Nursing course which drew a significant proportion of their students from overseas (mainly SE Asia). The course contains many technical terms such as medical terminology and nursing terms and was difficult for all students to adjust to. Our international students had additional problems. For example:

1. Adjusting to a different culture (Australian) with different attitudes, food and lifestyle. Students found it uncomfortable calling teachers by their first names and often used 'Madam' instead!

2. Adjusting to a pronunciation of English which differed from the pronunciation they were used to. For example, Korean students are often taught American English.

3. Adjusting to strict requirements regarding plagiarism which differed from their experience in their own countries.

The Vital English Pre-Arrival Learning programme was designed to alleviate some of these difficulties and has been used with success at British Columbia Centre for International Education through a webinar facility. The idea is for the institution to be able to make meaningful contact with overseas students before they arrive in the country where they will study. Students are guided through the orientation and registration process through a simulation which starts from the minute the plane arrives at the airport. They are shown the signs they must follow for passport control and then directed to the transport they need to take to get to their new university or college.

PAL courses benefit the institution as well. Students, and their families, are less anxious about their new environment. I remember the first group of Nepalese Nursing students who arrived at our college to study the Diploma of Nursing. Several of them explained that their families had to be convinced that it was safe for them to leave Nepal and to leave their families to study abroad.

Students who undertake a PAL programme demonstrate their level of English to the institution before arrival. This gives the institution a chance to put any learning support programmes in place before difficulties arise.

Duel Debate Module

Needs analysis is important for all courses and is especially important for the EMP area. EMP courses can cover a wide range of areas and must be targeted to students' needs.

Do you have any experience teaching English for Medical Purposes at a language school or as a pre-sessional course?

1. Yes, it was a positive experience and I got a lot out of it   or

2. Yes, it was a difficult experience and I was put off doing it again

Other English Language Specialities: LSP and CLIL

LSP or Language for Specific Purposes is an area of applied linguistics which is used in the teaching of specialised needs in any foreign language. The language which is focused on usually relates to a need for a job or study. Another use of the language is to research variations of language within a particular subject.

LSP in English is described as English for Specific Purposes or ESP. An example of the use of LSP is the common situation for doctors and nurses in the USA who find themselves needing to communicate with Spanish-speaking patients with poor Health Literacy, that is little knowledge of Medical English terms relating to their own health. In this case, the LSP is Spanish for Medical Purposes.

The second arm of LSP is the use in linguistic research. This is used in training for interpreting and translation and writing technical or specialised dictionaries, for example medical dictionaries. Medical dictionaries contain medical terms and also health-related or hospital-related terms. Some terms have an everyday equivalent which may have a different or slightly different meaning.

For example, in Medical English

'discharge' means either 'the secretions which ooze out of a wound' or 'patients leaving the hospital for home or transfer to another health facility'.

'observations' means 'vital signs and an overview of a patient's general status'

These are two words which have different meanings in a general sense.

LSP is contrasted with CBI or Content-based language instruction. Previously, CBI used to refer to the 'grammar-translation' method of teaching a foreign language which many of us (if you are over 40!) will be familiar with. The 'content', that is list of vocabulary words was presented at the beginning of the unit and followed by a translation passage which was probably written in an awkward style because it attempted to include as many examples of the grammar point of the particular unit. This resulted in many students saying that they had studied French for four years but were unable to make themselves understood when they actually landed in France and tried to order a meal!

These days, the term 'content' refers to the use of subject matter as a vehicle for second or foreign language learning. An example of this is the following Lesson Plan

Where Food Comes From

Students choose their favourite fruit and vegetable and classify whether it grows in cold or hot countries. Students classify vegetables as 'eaten cooked', 'eaten raw' and 'all of it is eaten'. Students can also classify fruit and vegetables as 'growing on trees', 'growing on bushes' or 'growing in the ground'.

Activities include: Apple Poem. Fruit quiz.

LANGUAGE: Names of fruit and vegetables, colours, sentence patterns 'Tomatoes are red; tomatoes grow on bushes.'

THINKING: Classifying types of food.

CBI teaching was officially sanctioned by the European Commission in 1995 when it was renamed CLIL or Content and Language Integrated Learning because it is language teaching which is integrated into the L1 or first language curriculum.

What is PAL?

PAL stands for Pre-Arrival Learning. Pre-Arrival Learning is something which most Colleges or Universities agree is extremely useful, however, few seem to offer. I used to teach in a Diploma of Nursing course which drew a significant proportion of their students from overseas (mainly SE Asia). The course contains many technical terms such as medical terminology and nursing terms and was difficult for all students to adjust to. Our international students had additional problems. For example:

1. Adjusting to a different culture (Australian) with different attitudes, food and lifestyle. Students found it uncomfortable calling teachers by their first names and often used 'Madam' instead!

2. Adjusting to a pronunciation of English which differed from the pronunciation they were used to. For example, Korean students are often taught American English.

3. Adjusting to strict requirements regarding plagiarism which differed from their experience in their own countries.

The Vital English Pre-Arrival Learning programme (www.vitalenglish.com/) was designed to alleviate some of these difficulties and has been used with success at British Columbia Centre for International Education (www.bccie.bc.ca/) through a webinar facility. The idea is for the institution to be able to make meaningful contact with overseas students before they arrive in the country where they will study. Students are guided through the orientation and registration process through a simulation which starts from the minute the plane arrives at the airport. They are shown the signs they must follow for passport control and then directed to the transport they need to take to get to their new university or college.

PAL courses benefit the institution as well. Students, and their families, are less anxious about their new environment. I remember the first group of Nepalese Nursing students who arrived at our college to study the Diploma of Nursing. Several of them explained that their families had to be convinced that it was safe for them to leave Nepal and to leave their families to study abroad.

Students who undertake a PAL programme demonstrate their level of English to the institution before arrival. This gives the institution a chance to put any learning support programmes in place before difficulties arise.

NMC should be able to test literacy   Published: 09 September 2011

The Royal College of Nursing has said the Nursing and Midwifery Council (NMC) should be able to test international registrants for English literacy to maintain high standards of care and patient safety.

In response to the Government's Green Paper Modernising the professional qualifications directive, Dr Peter Carter, the RCN's Chief Executive & General Secretary, said it is correct that nursing and other health professions have the right to be employed across the EU.

He said: "Patient safety will always be the top priority for nurses and other health care workers, so it is important that where certain standards and criteria are set, they are met by all staff, regardless of their background.

"The RCN believes that regulators, such as the NMC, should be able to test for language competency and that this requirement should be anchored in European law."

Dr Carter said UK nurses have to register every three years with the NMC and demonstrate their skills are up to date. However, the NMC is required to register a nurse from another EU country even if their skills are not up to date or they have not worked as a nurse for several years.

He added: "Equally, there is a responsibility placed on employers to ensure the language skills of all staff are of a high enough level to allow them to communicate effectively with patients and colleagues. Therefore, we would like to see checks in place to ensure continuing levels of competence for all health professionals.

"This is not to discriminate against nurses from any particular country, but rather to ensure the highest standards of care and patient safety are maintained and any barriers to that effect are removed."

Activity 1 : In pairs or groups, Share Your Knowledge

What ramifications would/will new regulations regarding language testing for EU nurses have for EMP teachers?

Who works in Health Care?

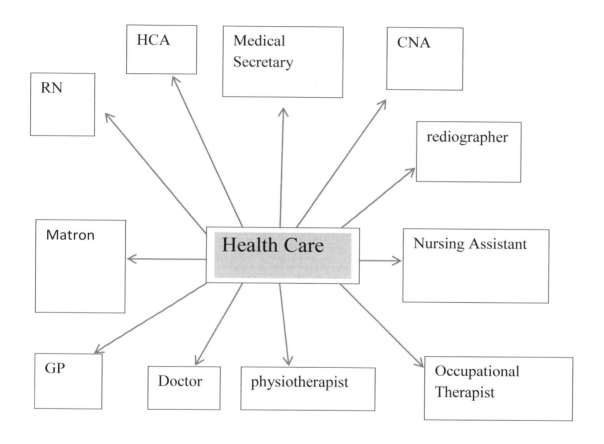

Suggestions for discussions:

- What level of language is appropriate to use with patients? Do patients want doctors and nurses to use medical terminology or everyday health terms?

- What is medical / nursing jargon? Why do doctors and nurses use jargon?

- What happens if healthcare workers use jargon with their patients?

Healthcare Workers

Teaching suggestions:

• Integrate with each body system e.g

Unit : The Heart

Specialists: cardiologist, cardiothoracic surgeon

• Integrate with medical terms for the topic ,e.g

cardio- heart

• Include the tests performed by the specialists in the particular area, e.g. ECG,

angiographer

Activity 2 : In pairs, describe the jobs these people do:

1. Cardiothoracic surgeon

2. CICU (Cardiac Intensive Care Unit) Nurse

3. Angiographer

4. Phlebotomist

Word Dynamo example

Using the Code of Ethics and the Code of Practice

http://www.nmc-uk.org/Publications/Standards/The-code/Introduction/

The code: Standards of conduct, performance and ethics for nurses and midwives

Chapters

• Introduction

• Make the care of people your first concern, treating them as individuals and respecting their dignity

• Work with others to protect and promote the health and wellbeing of those in your care, their families and carers, and the wider community

• Provide a high standard of practice and care at all times

• Be open and honest, act with integrity and uphold the reputation of your profession

• Information about indemnity insurance

• Contact

Suggestions:

- talking about responsibilities of nurses: discussion about different experiences of students

- talking about patient rights

- discussion about different hospital cultures e.g. role of doctor and nurse and involvement of patient in own care

- morals versus ethics

- 'Act with integrity' – implications for use of social media by healthcare workers

Compare the Nursing Code with the codes for doctors and physiotherapists.

What do you notice?

Common parts of the Codes

- Data Protection
- Confidentiality
- Access to health records
- Equality and research
- Record information accurately (objectively)
- Treat people as individuals / respect and dignity
- Informed consent
- Maintain professional boundaries

Powerpoint Slide: Healthcare Professionals by author

Compare notes on collecting and collating resources currently at the disposal of EMP trainers. This session seeks to identify and evaluate materials currently available to the trainer (course books as well as online) and other available resources and explores the challenges in their effective management. Input from course participants and teacher trainer alike promises an informative and practical workshop.

What resources are available for students and teachers?

I am going to concentrate on online resources here :

Vital English

www.vitalenglish.com/

has an excellent PAL Learning option as well as an online English for Medicine. According

to the website

PAL

Campus orientation

Comprehensive acculturation course

Individual study plan

English language course

English knowledge test (results emailed to you)

Multi-lingual registration

Progress tracking'

Speak IT English

www.speakitenglish.com

has an excellent online Pronunciation programme called 'Eye Speak English' . Pronunciation is an important part of EMP as the confusion of words through mispronunciation can have serious consequences.

CK Vocab Trainer

www.ck-translations.eu/

The Online Vocabulary Trainer. Don't be put off by the home page, select English as your language of choice and have a look at the Demo. There is a demo of heart terms using a translation from English to German but be aware that any language can be selected for translation.

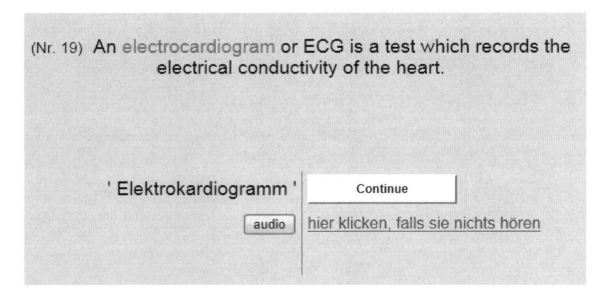

Medical English book publishers

Recently, many ELT publishers have included Medical English, for doctors and nurses in particular, in their ESP repertoire. Some of them have included Medical English titles in English in the Workplace series. Some have produced stand alone books.

Self publishing companies give authors the ability to self publish books which would otherwise be niche market books.

Cambridge University Press

Cambridge English for Nursing Pre-Intermediate by Virginia Allum and Patricia McGarr

Cambridge English for Nursing Intermediate Plus

Good Practice by Marie McCullagh and Ros Wright

Cambridge English for Nursing - Pre Int

by Virginia Allum and Patricia McGarr

Cambridge English for Nursing was written with the aim of supporting overseas nurses

who were starting work in the UK in particular. The book assumes a level of at least

Intermediate in order to cope with the technical vocabulary.

'Cambridge English for Nursing' could be classified as an LSP or Learning for Specific

Purposes book as it provides some of the specific terms needed to work as a nurse. LSP

materials are becoming more and more common as it is recognised that technical

vocabulary is an essential part of occupational English courses. The 'Cambridge

English for' books are all based around various occupations.

The topics covered in the Cambridge English for Nursing Pre-Intermediate book are:

Admitting patients

Caring for Patients after an operation

Caring for Terminally Ill Patients

The District Nurse

Helping Patients with Rehabilitation

Mobilising patients

Medical Imaging

Helping patients with diabetes management

Many of these areas are applicable to CNAs (Certified Nursing Assistants) or HCAs (Health Care Assistants) or Carers in Nursing Homes as well as nurses and nursing assistants in the hospital or community setting. There is a greater focus on bedside nursing in Cambridge English for Nursing Pre-Intermediate than in Cambridge English for Nursing Intermediate Plus which covers areas more commonly encountered by Registered Nurses.

Cambridge English for Nursing Intermediate Plus

by Virginia Allum and Patricia McGarr

The Cambridge English for Nursing Intermediate Plus was co-authored by myself and Patricia McGarr.

' Cambridge English for Nursing Intermediate Plus' is aimed at a higher level of English competency and covers some of the areas of nursing which are performed by Registered Nurses such as Patient Admissions

Respiratory problems

Wound Care

Diabetes Care

Medical Specimens

Medications

Intravenous infusions

Pre-operative patient assessment

Post-operative patient assessment

Discharge Planning

As with the Cambridge English for Nursing Pre-Intermediate Level book , there are 2 CD-ROMS as well as free online resources, such as the free Teachers Notes , free Medical Technology , free Glossaries and free Grammar Practice. Many of the larger publishers offer free on-line resources which complement the course books.

Good Practice

by Marie McCullagh and Ros Wright

Good Practice is one of the Medical English texts published by Cambridge University

Press. It pre-dates the English for Nursing texts as language support for doctors has a

longer history than English for Nursing. The book focuses on verbal communication

skills and has the added benefit of a DVD which enables better practice of non-verbal

communication skills. Patient interviews and assessments are often difficult skills for

overseas doctors to manage in English. Authentic and near authentic documents are

used to simulate the workplace and provide opportunity for rehearsal of common

scenarios.

Oxford University Press

Oxford University Press English for Careers is a series produced by Oxford University Press. Medical and Nursing English are both represented in the series. Both 'Oxford English for Careers: Nursing' and 'Oxford English for Careers: Medicine' have two levels of ability.

Pearson Longman

Pearson English for Nursing has the distinction of having a grammar focus as well as a specialist vocabulary focus. The CD-ROM reinforces pronunciation of the terms in the glossary.

Level 1: CEF level A1 to A2

Level 2: CEF level A2 to B1'

Garnet Education

<u>English for Medicine in Higher Education Studies</u> by Patrick Fitzgerald, Marie McCullagh and Ros Wright was written for medical students who are preparing to enter university. The Garnet book differs from the previous examples as it has an academic focus and offers practice in the development of the sort of skills which students will need to listen to lectures and write essays.

This is another arm of EMP which is sometimes called LSP (Learning for Specific Purposes) as the focus is on the specific need for academic medical skills.

LAP Lambert Academic Publishing

Lambert Academic Publishing offers to publish some of the millions of academic theses which are written every year. They also publish academic articles and research notes so that the authors' wealth of knowledge and experience is not lost after completion of Further Education studies.

Cengage Learning

'English for Health Sciences' by Kristin L. Johannsen, Martin Milner, Josephine O'Brien, Hector Sanchez, Ivor Williams is a workplace focussed text. Topics such as 'putting a patient at ease with small talk, taking a medical history and asking open-ended questions' are used to help students practise real life situations. Many EMP authors agree that one of the best ways for students to increase their confidence in language skills is to rehearse relevant language in a simulated workplace environment.

Springer

Springer is a major publisher in the scientific and medical fields. Medical English is written from the perspective of a Medical Officer and includes advice on workplace issues such as acronyms and 'Latin' terminology. The authors also deal with topics such as avoiding common English mistakes and, unusually, a 'sightseeing conversation guide'.

The authors, Ramón Ribes and Pablo Ros also teamed up to write 'Radiological English' which is unique in dealing with a very specialised area, radiology. Most often specialities like radiology are viewed as niche markets and not taken on by publishers who often fear that the financial return will be too low.

Express Publishing

Express Publishing is a small, independent publishing house which only publishes ELT or English Language Teaching materials. The English for Nursing text is 'Career Paths English: Nursing' by Virginia Evans and Kori Salcido.

The English for Doctors text is by Virginia Evans, Jenny Dooley and Trang M. Tran, M.D. Both editions have UK and US versions including UK and US audio versions.

Verlag Hans Huber

Nursing English Essentials is a bilingual English for Nursing text which includes a German/ English glossary.

Schenk Verlag

<u>English for Doctors</u> was written for doctors, medical students and nurses. It covers 13 areas of medicine which is many more than most other EMP texts. The layout of the book is very compact with little white space and can appear a little overwhelming. Despite this, the book has been well researched with a substantial advisory team.

Online Resources

Free teaching and learning resources for Medical English

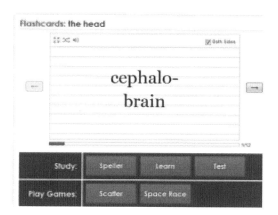

Blended Learning is the buzz word (or words) of today. Online resources can help make teaching and learning a lot easier. All the better as the following examples are free. Some, like the Cambridge University Press resources are offered as a goodwill gesture to support the materials which teachers and learners may have already bought. They are also a great marketing tool if the resource directs a teacher or learner to buy the book which goes with the resource.

Some of the resources provide practice in areas which may not have been covered or covered slightly in the book they refer to. In the case of 'Cambridge English for Nursing', for example, the bulk of the practice in the books was aimed at verbal communication. There was not a lot of time devoted to written communication, although it was covered in each unit. The Medical Technology resources gave us the opportunity to offer some reading texts which we thought were current and interesting and would stimulate discussion as well.

Some resources are interactive activities such as click and drag or matching activities. Some of these activities may be on a site which offers you the opportunity to either access resources made and donated by others or to make your own. An example of one of these is the Quizlet website.

I always think that it's always a nice idea to share your resources with colleagues and learners.

Cambridge University Press website

Cambridge English for Nursing complete package of free resources linked to the two Cambridge English for Nursing books. The Teachers Notes are available for all units of both books as well as additional teaching resources for Medical Technology, Glossaries and Grammar Practice

TEFL net

The TEFLtastic Medical English worksheets is a wonderful list of resources .

English Med

The English Med website, englishmed is ' an initiative of Elanguest sponsored by the European Union's Leonardo Da Vinci project. The Leonardo da Vinci Programme was set up to fund vocational education projects such as training opportunities or larger scale ventures.

The Englishmed project produced medical language practice for doctors, nurses and pharmacists. Simple cartoon figures are used in the short video clips which model the dialogues.

Hospital English.com

HospitalEnglish.com contains many free Medical English teaching materials. There are both worksheets and lesson plans for teachers on the site. Topics covered include discussions of diseases such as asthma, diabetes and arthritis and discussion of treatment and procedures. The website offers practice in reading comprehension as well as vocab building.

QUIA

Quia 'is pronounced key-ah, and is short for Quintessential Instructional Archive. Quia provides tools which can be used by teachers to make their own resources by using the templates on the site. Alternatively, teachers or learners can use resources which have been shared for everyone's use. The Medicine category has almost one hundred activities to choose from. Rank no 1 is 'Directional Terms' and no 2 is 'Medical Terminology'. Well worth checking through to revise terms or set as homework.

Sheppard Software

This was a real find! On the Sheppard Software website, you'll find the Learn Medical terminology game. Click to play and try out your knowledge. As you answer, a voice gives you feedback.

There are apparently 340 questions in all. Each quiz picks 20 questions at random.

Squidoo Featured Lenses: Virginia Allum

Squidoo is a self-publishing outlet where 'lensmasters' make 'lenses' which are in

effect webpages. Links can be made to Amazon and other websites.

www.squidoo.com

English for Doctors

English for Medical Purposes: Doctors covers the sorts of communication skills doctors

need to ensure that they can talk with their patients and colleagues...

Tips for Teaching Medical Terminology

Medical terminology is the specialised vocabulary used by healthcare workers to

describe parts of the body, procedures, medical equipment and instruments. M...

More Tips for Teaching Medical Terminology

Medical Terminology is a wide subject to teach and involves using a lot of strategies to

make it less dry. It is important for doctors and nurses to have a...

EMP - English for Medical Purposes

English for Medical Purposes is one of the areas of ESP or English for Specific

Purposes. Recently it has become clear that specialised knowledge in healthc...

English for Healthcare Assistants

Health Care Assistants are also known as Certified Nursing Assistants. Often seen as

the backbone of the healthcare industry. They provide practical bedside...

Top 5 Tips for Student Nurses

Last assignment handed in, last prac attended so it's time to start on the next learning

phase.Your first job will be a steep learning curve which many nurs...

Link List

EMP Tokyo Medical University www.emp-tmu.net/

Really comprehensive site which includes reading materials for 3rd and 4th year medical students and also videos with transcripts covering different diseases and conditions. Registration and log in required.

All Nurses Forum www.allnurses.com/

A list of links published on the All Nurses Forum. There are a variety of procedures shown e.g peripheral cannulation.

Free medical Terminology Exercises

www.medterminologyforcare.co.uk/medical/free-interactive-medical-terminology-exercises.htm

great list of free exercises, review first then test yourself. You can pick the British English or U.S English option before you start

Isothermal Community College website www.isothermal.edu/library/medterm.htm

another great list of useful links in itself. The resources aim to support the courses provided at the college but have obvious wider applications

Sheppard Software Online Games

www.sheppardsoftware.com/web_games_vocab_med.htm

The 'Learn Terminology' section has a large set of questions which are randomly selected for the online quiz. Immediate feedback. There is no pronunciation of terms, however, a computer-generated voice tells you if you are right or not

Medical Terminology Activities

www.msjensen.cehd.umn.edu/1135/med_term_activites/

This is useful for students and teachers of EMP. Teachers may like to re-work these on line worksheets as a paper worksheet, perhaps mixing prefix and suffix activities.

Alternatively, students can access the site and do the activities on line. There's a lot of reinforcement of terms and examples of terms. For instance, one question asks the prefix meaning under and gives a clue with the expressions (-clavian artery, -arachnoid space). The level is quite high and presupposes an understanding of anatomy and physiology terms.

TEFL Net www.tefl.net/

A great site for resources for teaching English as a Foreign Language. The site has a broad range of resources including quizzes, activities, worksheets and even lesson plans. You can do much more than that! The Medical English section, hosted by Alex Case, is called TEFLTastic and it truly is. Great activities for both medical and pharma students.

Breaking News English - 10,000 Germ Species In/On Our Body

www.breakingnewsenglish.com/1206/120615-germs.html

This is one of the free worksheets on Breaking News English, a nice site with a great variety of news 'bites'. This one is about the microbes in our bodies. A lesson plan is included with everything needed for pair work activities. The only thing I could not find was the audio for the listening activity, however, it relates to the written text so it should not be a problem. Not aimed above B1 level but with the potential for extension work for more able students.

Medical English difficult sounds pairwork worksheets

www.tefl.net/alexcase/worksheets/medical-pharmaceutical-english/medical-sounds-pairwork/

This is a very nice free resource from Alex Case. It encourages students to speak in groups and describe medical terms. From a practical point of view, it has a wide application in everyday communication with patients and colleagues e.g. explaining to a patient what a piece of equipment does

HospitalEnglish - Arthritis www.hospitalenglish.com/students/arthritis.php

One of the free resources on Hospital English. There is a Student version and a Teacher version. What I like about the resource is that the initial word list has clickable audio of each term which is clear and not too 'computer-generated'. There is also audio for the Listening activity (well, there would be!) and also audio of the reading text. I did find a typo in Article 1 ('bodyfs' instead of 'body's') but this should not affect understanding of the text. I would judge the level to be at B1 with a reasonable number of the medical terms needed to discuss arthritis.

EFL Laboratory- Medical terminology activities

www.amarris.homestead.com/vocabactivities.html

This site has a range of activities for students in the health sciences e.g medicine and pharmaceuticals. There are also activities in the areas of Chemistry, Biology and Physics. I looked at the activities in the medical terminology section and found some crosswords which are great practice for recycling medical terms.

Englishmed- surgery www.englishmed.com/general-staff/dialogue-26/

This is one of the activities on the Englishmed site which offers practice in Medicine, Nursing, Pharmacy and Surgery. The short video clips use stick figure characters to role play the dialogues which can be read alongside the cartoon window. The dialogues have exercises as well.

English Talking - Living with Breast Cancer www.english-talking-medicine.com/medical-interviews-listening-exercises.html

This is an example of the activities available on the English Talking site. The accent is British English, however, the content is applicable to any Medical English course. The listening text is very long, however, it is broken into manageable sections

University of Bath - medical English activities

www.bath.ac.uk/elc/eap/health/index.htm

There are five topics in the Health section of short activities. Both the 'I caught a cold' and 'How to give artificial respiration' have reordering activities. These appear to be the only free resources as the Medical English exercises require a log in. The level is B1. Good practice for eventual communication of the steps of a process e.g. I'm going to (do a dressing, do an ECG etc) . First, I'll..Then I'll ..

Session 4: Developing Activities for Medical English Vocabulary

What do EMP students need to know?

- specialised vocabulary

- medical terminology

- acronyms and abbreviations

- medical and nursing jargon

- everyday health language

What do stakeholders i.e hospital employers expect?

- Ability of nurses to communicate effectively

- Safe practice and high standards of technical knowledge

- Cultural sensitivity and awareness

- Good teamwork

- Ability to work with other Health Care Professionals e.g doctors, physios

But they still need..

- General reading skills (sentence and paragraph structure, skimming and scanning)

- General writing skills (writing statements, writing letters, using abbreviations and acronyms)

- Functional communication language

And other useful language like...

- Clarifying 'Can I check whether phlebotomy means the same as venepuncture?

- Asking for repetition ' Could you repeat that term please? I didn't hear you.'
- Explaining lack of understanding 'I don't understand what that means. Could you please explain it to me again?'

Complicating factors

- Some students are <u>very</u> low level
- Some curricula spread few teaching hours over 6 semesters
- little time to develop language skills
- Need realistic learning goals which can lead to further consolidation

The Upside..

- EMP Students who are qualified doctors/nurses etc have background knowledge and terms in own language
- Medical terminology and related terms are similar in many languages
- EMP is useful and relevant to medical/nursing students in their L1 course

Learning Medical terminology

- A lot of memory work!
- Word parts often from Latin or Greek (new languages for some)
- Good news: many word parts are recycled in several terms
- Many terms similar to terms in own language

Remind students that

- Memorising is a big part of learning medical terminology

- 'Learning by heart' means learning how the word looks and sounds and putting it in context

- Learn no more than 5 new terms a day

- Use (say aloud) new terms frequently

- Encourage students to make their own notebook of new terms , translate if needed

- Include pronunciation e.g from www.thefreedictionary.com

- A-Z terms or Terms for each System of the Body

- Use medical terminology games each lesson to revise terms or provide worksheets for students to practise at home (in pairs)

- Think about developing a website for each course e.g on Wix . Students contribute their own activities to the site. Develop a forum on the site.

  Example of a Wix

Authorsden article : What kind of glossary development will help EMP students become more confident

by Virginia Allum

When reading and writing medical and nursing texts, Health Care Professionals require an understanding of medical and hospital terminology in the first instance. As well as this, Health Care Professionals need to be able to write fluently in patient notes, in referral letters and when completing care plans or care pathways. Finally, they need to be able to communicate information in writing about patient status and changes in patient condition. Most course books for doctors or nurses concentrate on improving verbal and listening skills and often only touch on writing skills which are needed in the workplace. This is usually because the books are written from an ELT perspective which scorns the teaching of 'content'. Of course, I'm not suggesting that English for nurses or doctors aims to equip students to pass a medical or nursing degree, however, I believe there is a need to help establish a glossary of hospital terms so that the workplace is less daunting when they finally make it!

The kind of writing which doctors and nurses undertake at work is different from the academic writing of essays which practitioners would have been familiar with as undergraduates. Much of the writing is formulaic. In the case of nurses; nurses complete care plans and care pathways which have a limited amount of prose writing and have a greater amount of tick boxing and short phrase writing instead. They read short phrases about patient care, for example ' Pt mobilising with/without mobility aid' and initial when the milestone is achieved.

This is not to say that there is no writing of complete sentences and/or paragraphs. Variances in the patient's ability to reach a goal or milestone is documented in the care pathway with an explanation. Referral letters to outside agencies for after care e.g after discharge home are written as mini reports.

There is an increasing need for nursing and medical graduates to publish papers and present at conferences so correct spelling especially of medical terms is essential. Medical or hospital language can be divided into:

- medical terminology

- medical and nursing jargon - used between colleagues

- everyday health terms – used in discussions with patients

- terms relating to equipment or procedures – collocations often used with these

By exploring groups of 'headwords' in medicine, larger glossaries can be developed which help students learn the immense corpora of medical terms they need to know to function at high levels of language. There are many compound words in Medicine particularly relating to new discoveries e.g *stem cell research*. By adding to a solid base of headwords, students gradually become aware of terms which 'go together'. This is a mark of fluency and helps with comprehensibility. It also helps to reduce the number of completely new terms which need to be learned.

Development of Medical Terminology Glossary

Tips for learning medical Terminology

http://www.squidoo.com/tips-for-teaching-medical-terminology

Learning Medical Terminology doesn't have to be mind-numbing

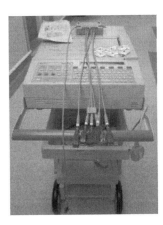

Medical terminology is the specialised vocabulary used by healthcare workers to describe parts of the body, procedures, medical equipment and instruments. Medical terms are made up of two or three parts which may come from several languages apart from English. The most common languages are Latin and Greek.

There are several thousand medical terms in use, many of which fortunately share common prefixes or suffixes. Learning medical terms requires quite a lot of memorizing which many students find tedious so it is a good idea for teachers to use a variety of activities for students to be able to revise and review the terms in a fun way.

How much do you know about medical terminology?

There are rules for making the medical terms which refer to medical equipment, diseases and disorders and medical procedures. Once you learn the rules you are able to make many different medical terms by recycling the medical terminology building blocks.

How much do you know about how medical terms are made?

○ Not a lot, I know the names of a few diseases and some medical equipment from personal experience

○ A little bit. I know they are made up of different prefixes and suffixes.

○ A little bit. I know that each term has a main part which is changed by adding different prefixes or suffixes

○ Quite a bit ,I have a medical background

○ Hardly anything but I'm willing to learn!

How are medical terms built?

Medical terms are made up of several parts which may come from several languages apart from English. The most common languages are Latin and Greek.

There are several thousand medical terms in use, many of which fortunately share common prefixes or suffixes. Learning medical terms requires quite a lot of memorizing which many students find tedious so it is a good idea for teachers to use a variety of activities for students to be able to revise and review the terms in a fun way.

Most medical terms consist of one or more parts. These parts may be:

Prefixes - the part which goes in front of the base word

Base word - also called the root word. This is often the term for a part of the body e.g. cardio- the heart. Some terms have more than one baseword

Suffix - the part which goes at the end of the base word

Joining vowel - often 'o' . The vowel is added so that the medical term flows better

An example of a medical term is the word Electrocardiograph.

It can be broken down into the following parts:

electro (prefix) + cardio (baseword) + graph (suffix)

'electrical' + ' heart' + 'a recording of something'

electrocardiograph = recording of the electrical function of the heart

Many prefixes and suffixes are used again and again, so once learned they can be reused in different terms. For example,

hypo- low hypothermia (low temperature) hypoglycaemia (low blood sugar) hyponatraemia (low sodium) hypoxia (low oxygen)

Overview of medical terms

Medical terminology Describing the processes of the body	The Systems of the Body People in hospital	Describing diseases and conditions Describing surgical interventions
Cardiovascular System Cardio- Corono- Sino- Atrio- Ventriculo- heart Atria Ventricles Aorta Tricuspid valve Mitral valve	ECG CABG Blood pressure EBP	Angina Atherosclerosis , Hypertension, Myocardial Infarction Anaemia
Haematological system Arterio- Veno- Phlebo- Vasculo- Vaso- Haem- -aemia Blood vessels Artery Vein Capillary blood	Angiogram Text: radiology text e.g. contrast consent	Cerebrovascular accident Phlebitis Haemorrhage anaemia
Respiratory System Pneumo- Pleura- Pulmono- Trachea Bronchi- pharynx larynx trachea lungs pleura bronchi alveoli	Tracheotomy Oxygen therapy Bronchodilators Text: Pharmacological: drug info leaflet	pleuritis pneumonia bronchitis Asthma COPD
Nervous system Cerebro- Encephalo- Neuro- Myelo- Brain Nerve meninges	Myelogram EEG Text: Post procedure (myelogram) instructions	Cerebrovascular Event/Accident (CVE/CVA) neuritis
Digestive system - GIT	Gastroscopy	pharyngitis

Oro- Glosso- Linguo- Oesophago- Gastro- Naso Pharyngo- Laryngo- Mouth nose Pharynx Larynx Oesophagus Epiglottis stomach	Endoscopy Text: Radiology Endoscope features	gastritis peptic ulcer
Digestive system - Liver and gallbladder Hepato- Icto- Cholecysto- Liver gallbladder	Cholecystectomy Cholangiogram Text: Medicine: Laparoscopy / Minimally invasive surgery	Jaundice Hepatitis cholecystitis
Digestive system - Lower GIT Duodeno- Jejuno- Ileo- Small intestine Duodenum Jejunum ileum	Ileostomy Colostomy Text: colostomy aids	Duodenal ulcer
Digestive system - Lower GIT Colo- Recto- Ano- Large intestine Colon Rectum anus	Colonoscopy	Text: Medical: Cancer of the colon Colorectal cancer Anal fistula
Musculo-skeletal system Osteo- Osso- Arthro- Ortho- teno- musculo- Bone joint tendon muscle	Arthrodesis R.I.C.E Arthroscopy Text: Physiotherapy: post-op exercises	Osteoporosis arthritis
Integumentary System	Subcutaneous injection	Dermatitis

Cutaneo- Dermo- Skin	Text: Protocol for continuous subcutaneous infusion	
Special Senses- sight Oculo- Opto- Ophthalmo- Eye Conjunctiva retina	optometrist ophthalmic surgery	retinal detachment Text: Testing for glaucoma conjunctivitis
Special Senses - hearing Tympano- Auro- Labyrinth- Ear Tympanic membrane	Aural testing Text: Audiometry Testing for hearing loss	labyrinthitis
Renal System Reno- Nephro- Cysto- Ureto- Urethra- Urino- Kidneys Bladder Ureter urethra	Urinary catheter Text: Intermittent Self Catheterisation catheters	Renal colic nephritis UTI
Female reproductive Salpingo- Oophero- Ovaro- Utero- Hystero- Mammo- Uterus Ovaries Fallopian tubes	Hysterectomy Ovarian cancer	salpingitis
Male reproductive Testiculo- Peno- Prostato- Epidydimo- Penis Testes Prostate Epidydimus	TURP Text: Intermittent bladder irrigation	Prostatitis Testicular cancer
Endocrine system Endocrino- Exocrino-	Glucometer Text: Diabetes Personal Care Plan	Pancreatitis Insulinoma Hyperglycaemia

Pancreato- Insulin- Gluco- Glycol- pancreas		hypoglycaemia
Endocrine system Adeno- hypophysis Pineal gland Pituitary Thymus ADH	Text: antidiuretic therapy dehydration	Diabetes Insipidus
Endocrine system Adreno- Thyro- Adrenal Thyroid Parathyroid	Text: TH3 and TH4 testing	Hypothyroidism Cushings Syndrome
Behavioural Medicine Psycho- Psycologico- brain	Text: Non pharmacological measures used in dementia	Dementia Bipolar Disorder Schizophrenia

Developing authentic materials for English for Medical Purposes classes

Let's start by using 'Wound Care' as an example. You can use any other medical or nursing procedure in its place.

Aims of the lesson are to:

present the specialised language needed to talk about wounds. Tip: look at wound websites which often give advice to professionals on the use of the dressings.

review prefixes and suffixes used to describe the skin, blood vessels (vascular) and blood

recycle general English e.g asking for information, giving advice, assessing pain, giving directions

use maths terms e.g dimensions of wound, amount of discharge

The lesson should prepare dialogues which students can role play in the class-room and later at home. A word about role plays - They are serious enough for ESP! They are the perfect opportunity to use specialised language in authentic situations as they can be used for hand overs , telephone calls and conversations with colleagues.

Students can write their own role plays and then feel that they 'own' them. Think about bringing in guest speakers e.g real nurses or doctors to confirm the authenticity of the role plays,

Talking about Wound Care gives an opportunity for:

Verbal descriptions e.g. in handover

Written descriptions e.g. Wound Chart

Abbreviations and medical terminology

Description of Equipment e.g Dressings

Practice of Documentation: Care pathways

A review of staff who work in Wound Care e.g Infection Control Nurse, Tissue Viability Nurse

What can you say about wounds?

Make this a 'Before you start.' section. Brainstorm the following areas to see how much students already know about the topic.

1. Types of wounds - surgical, ulcers, lacerations

2. Position on body - on the right ankle

3. Description - order of adjectives

4. Colour - of the surrounding skin, wound discharge

5. Size - width and depth

6. Amount of exudate - small, moderate, copious

As you can see, there are some good practice areas for students which will be useful for other areas, for example

Position : use of prepositions

Description: order of adjectives

Size : use of mathematical terms

For extended practice, put your class into 6 groups and allocate one of the 6 areas to each group. Get students to make flashcards or an activity (e.g. adjective order activity) so the whole class can build up their knowledge of the terms. Reassure students that the vocabulary used to talk about Wound Care is extensive and will be learned gradually.

Other areas of Wound Care which can be covered with advanced classes are:

Presence and type of wound drains

Specialised Wound Care Equipment e.g VAC Dressings

Equipment used to do a dressings e.g surgical tape, bandages

Types of skin closures: sutures, clips, staples and Steristrips

Everyday terms versus medical term (healing v granulating)

Parts of the Body

Use diagrams or photos of the body for students to talk about where wounds are situated.

Practise:

Terminology (body position - anterior, posterior etc) - on the back of..

Parts of the body e.g where pressure ulcers may occur - on her sacrum

Everyday terms versus medical terminology - shoulder blade - scapula

Using authentic diagrams

If you can get hold of authentic charts or documents from your local hospital or online, use them for students to complete for a pretended wound. For example, a man was bitten by a dog and has a wound here It's a cut (what is the medical term? = laceration) . He has left it for a couple of days and there is now pus in it (purulent=pussy). It's painful all the time.

An example of a scenario for students to use. Students read the scenario, complete a wound care chart and then write a dialogue of a handover. During the handover they will hand over the information about the patient to the next shift.

Mr D Hatworth was repairing his fence when he accidentally dropped a piece of wood which grazed his right lower leg. He left the wound untreated for two weeks apart from dabbing on a bit of antiseptic cream. Now, the wound is painful to touch and is red and inflamed. There is a small amount of blood-stained discharge

Make your own flashcards

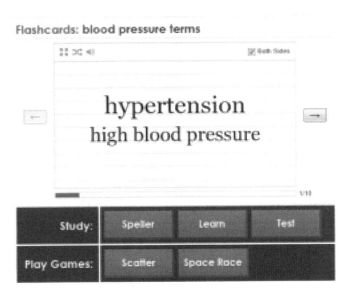

There are some great, free flashcard generators online. One I've used is on <u>Quizlet</u> . It's as simple as typing in the terms on a particular theme -the one I tried was 'Blood Pressure' which is available to anyone on the quizlet site. The software automatically generates the flashcards which are double sided and have audio associated with each card. A word of caution - the pronunciation is U.S pronunciation which can vary from UK pronunciation particularly in the way words are stressed. I noticed this in the pronunication of 'asystole' which I would pronounce as a-sys-tol-e. The flashcard pronunciation was a-sys-tole.

You, the teacher, can make your own flashcards which you then ask students to try online (registration is free on the site) or share flashcards already produced on a topic you are unfamiliar with.

Ask students to make their own set and then share with class-mates

Lower level students can prepare terms in class so that you can be sure of the accuracy. Then, they can make the flashcards at home. It is important that you check the information before the flashcards are made or incorrect terms or meanings will be learned.

Use the flashcards as a pair-work exercise. Students do another student's flashcards

Another excellent feature of this programme is the ability to generate other related activities such as multiple-choice questions. These can be done online with the benefit of instant feedback to the student.

Make your own crosswords

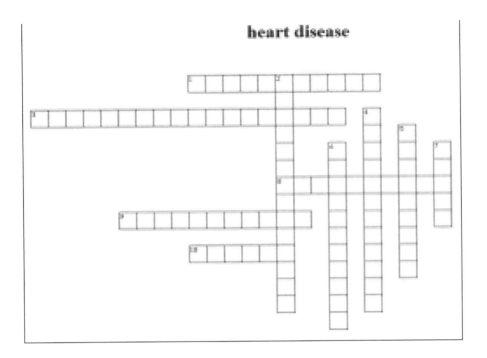

heart disease

Recycling medical terms through cross words is another great activity especially as a homework exercise or a Friday afternoon exercise. I have used a free crossword generator from Puzzlemaker . Crosswords generated on Puzzlemaker, called 'Criss Cross', are simplified crosswords which can be used to recycle language studied during the previous week.

It is also possible to make cryptograms on this site. Add the clues and answers and the puzzle is automatically generated as a pdf which can be printed out for students to use. A word of caution: only use single words in the clues or write compound words as one word. For example, blood pressure needs to be written as 'bloodpressure' because the puzzle generator only recognises single terms. If compound terms are written with the space , the second term will be included in the clues. In the case of 'blood pressure', only 'blood' will be in the actual puzzle and 'pressure' will be found in the clue.

Create matching activities and clozes

Tools For English

The Tools For English website is a real teacher's pal. There are several ,free tools which you (or your students) can use to generate activities which help to recycle language. Not only are the activities generated (as pdfs which can be printed) but there is also the facility to generate answer sheets. A real godsend.

The sort of activities you can make are:

Gap Fill activities

Filtering Activities (filter modals, prepositions, verbs)

Scrambling activities (use them to scramble articles using medical terms)

Matching activities (match medical term with equivalent everyday term e.g myocardial infarction - heart attack)

True /False

Multiple choice questions

All activities can be used to practise aspects of medical terminology learning:

terms in context (use cloze, scrambling)

understanding of the everyday equivalent term - this is very important for doctors and nurses to be able to explain procedures to patients

Multiple choice questions - this is also good practice for nursing exams such as the RN-NCLEX

Use blended learning options

English 360

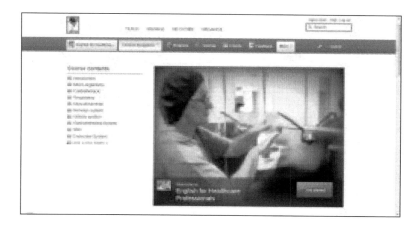

Think about using an LMS such as English 360 to add value to your teaching. It also opens the way to pulling in trusted resources to your course and gives students an opportunity to become independent learners.

English360 is free for freelance teachers and authors. You are only charged an access fee when students start using English360. English360 is a pay-as-you-go service; the cost is paid monthly with a limit of 9 students.

Blended learning works best when it works in with classroom learning rather than standing alone as an extra. The benefit of f2f teaching and classroom camaraderie cannot be dismissed, however, blended learning adds a different perspective to your teaching and may appeal to the learning styles of your students.

More Tips for Teaching medical Terminology

http://www.squidoo.com/more-tips-for-teaching-medical-terminology

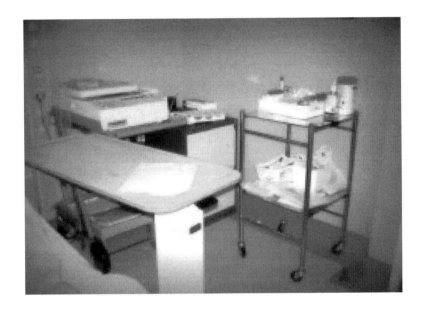

Medical Terminology is a wide subject to teach and involves using a lot of strategies to make it less dry. It is important for doctors and nurses to have a good grasp of medical terms and everyday equivalent terms. In some languages e.g. Spanish, French, Italian and Portuguese, medical terms are well understood by both healthcare workers and patients alike. In English, however, everyday terms are more commonly used by patients.

Doctors and nurses should make sure that they use the level of language used by patients when explaining procedures and illnesses. This ensures that communication barriers are not set up between health worker and patient. At the same time, they need to be able to use medical terms when speaking to colleagues or writing in hospital notes.

Making tagxedos

Use the <u>Tagxedo</u> website to make unusual containers for your word clouds. I made an example in the shape of a heart - it contains many expressions relating to the heart and heart disease. Ask students to identify as many terms as possible. Students write them in a list and then explain their meaning to their partner. Students can form their own tagxedos using the templates available.

Prefix Charades

ENDO <small>WITHIN</small>	**HYPO** <small>LOW</small>
SUB <small>UNDER</small>	**HYPER** <small>HIGH</small>
PERI <small>AROUND</small>	**TACHY** <small>FAST</small>

Getting students to perform activities which require them to be <u>active</u> is a good idea. Moving around the room or performing actions, gets the brain going and helps in memory work. Prefix Charades can easily be made using a simple table with six sections. Write or type the prefix in large letters and include the meaning in very small letters if needed. Cut out the sections and make single cards. These can be laminated if they are to be re-used several times. Hand out a card to one student who acts out the prefix. Explain that no words may be used. For example, the prefix 'sub' (under) could be acted as 'putting an object under a table'. The rest of the class tried to guess the prefix. The successful student takes the place of the first student and takes another card. As the prefix is guessed correctly ,the teacher writes the prefix and meaning on the whiteboard.

Mind maps

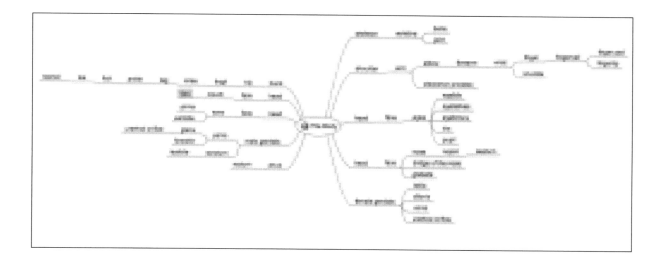

Mind maps give students a chance to chunk together information which belongs together. The free software FreeMind allows you and your students to develop mindmaps.

Starting with a central idea, e.g. 'human <u>body</u>' , side sections are added to the central idea. I made a mind map of the human body and filled in as many everyday terms as I could think of. The mind map could be used by removing some of the terms which students need to replace. Students could also include the medical term for each everyday term e.g.over the everyday term 'skull', students would write 'cranium'.

Column Sorting activities

Heart/ Blood/ Diseases/Medication

Instructions: Sort the items from the box into the appropriate column.

heart	blood	disease/condition	medication

Column sorting activities can be used to place terms under different categories. There are several different programmes which teachers can use to make the activity online. I used one from TEFL Net. Alternatively, tables can be set up offline.

Give students a list of terms which need to be put under the correct heading. For example:

1. Headings - prefix , base word, suffix

2. Headings - equipment, operations , diseases

3. Headings - prefixes for colour , prefixes for size , suffixes for size or shape

Use photos of self and family

Make labelling activities easily using your own photos.

Parts of the body

Position of the body

Movement of the body

Picture labelling activities

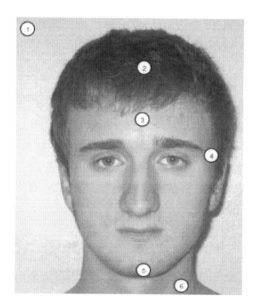

Use authentic pictures or pictures which you have permission to use. Add labels to parts of the body. I used a photo of my son (to avoid problems with consent!) .I have added numbered dots for students to label. Teachers can insert the photo into a worksheet ,add a box of terms for students to use to label the photo. For example:

Use the following terms to label the photo below:

cervix caput- mandible frontis- tricho- temporalis

Then, students can label the photo with everyday terms:

head   hair   forehead   temple   lower jaw   neck

Squidoo: Where do medical words come from?

http://www.squidoo.com/where-do-medical-words-come-from

Interesting medical words staring with 'A'

Many medical terms come to us from other languages. A large number come from Ancient Greek and Latin but also from Arabic as the great trail-blazers of anatomy came from these civilisations. Hippocrates, Galen and Abu al-Qasim al-Zahrawi, 'the father of modern surgery' all contributed to the knowledge base of anatomy and physiology which we have today.

Many everyday medical terms came to us from Anglo - Saxon words. These often tend to be words relating to the outside of the body e.g. hand, shoulder ,elbow.

Some of the terms come from words which describe things which we know are inaccurate e.g 'artery' . The words had already become so well established that they weren't changed and they remain as oddities today..

What is medical etymology?

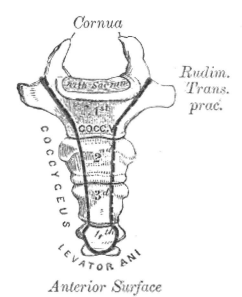

Medical etymology is the linguistic origin of medical words and terms. 'Etymology' comes from 'etymom' , a Greek word which means 'the true meaning of' + logy meaning word.

Etymology looks back at the development of a word from its original language through any other languages it comes up against. This may happen during the conquest of a country and its people especially if the conquest moves into settlement. An example of this is the movement of Latin words into the English language after the Roman conquest and then mixing of Roman and Briton populations.

Medical etymology is interesting because many medical terms come from the Greek or Latin because the Ancient Greeks and then the Romans were keen anatomists. The early terms for any parts of the body which look like everyday articles ended up with medical terms which may appear a little strange. For example, the coccyx bone is named after the Greek word for a cuckoo because they thought it resembled the shape of a cuckoo's beak.

Other languages have also contributed to medical terminology. The languages include Arabic, Chinese, Dutch, French, Gaelic, German, Hindu, Italian, Japanese, Persian, Portuguese and Spanish. The names of researchers or physicians who were instrumental in the discovery of a disease or condition are also included in medical etymology.

How well do you know your -ologies?

1. What is entomology?

- ○ A. the study of the intestines

- ○ B. the study of insects

- ○ C. the study of medical instruments

2. What is semantics?

- ○ A. The study of the shape of words

- ○ B. The study of the sound of words

- ○ C. The study of the meaning of words

acetabulum

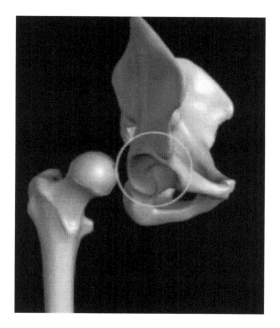

Comes from the Latin word 'acetum' which means vinegar and the suffix -bulum which means 'instrument'. It is described as the cup-shaped cavity at the base of the hipbone into which the head of the femur fits. The cupped part of the hip bone looked like a vinegar cruet which was commonly used in Roman times.

These days, the acetabulum may be replaced with a metal prothesis during a hip replacement operation.

To remember the term 'acetum', think of 'acetic acid' which is found in vinegar.

Hip Replacement

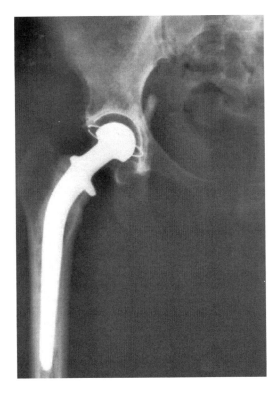

The first step of a hip replacement surgery is to remove the damaged cartilage and bone in the hip. The hip consists of the head of the femur (the ball part) and the acetabulum (socket). That is why the hip is called a 'ball and socket ' joint. In a person suffering from arthritis (arthro=joint + -itis =inflammation of), the surface of the hip wears away and the ball and socket joint starts to crumble causing pain especially when walking or exercising.

Before an orthopaedic surgeon can put in a replacement joint, the old ball and socket and worn cartilage needs to be scooped out. The ball part of the joint can be cut off but the acetabulum forms part of the pelvis so can't be removed. The acetabulum is ground down to remove the damaged cartilage and bone. The surface is smoothed to make it ready for the metal hip replacement prosthesis which forms a cup-like structure. The prosthesis is hammered into the smooth cup which is formed and after a while bone grows over the prosthesis to hold it in place.

Achilles heel

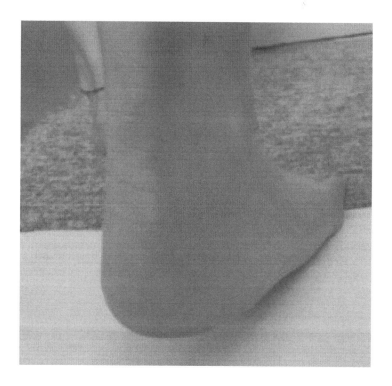

The word Achilles refers to the Greek child ,Achilles whose mother dipped him into the river Styx by his mother to protect him from wounds. Because she held him by his heel, his heel was not protected and became his 'weak point' . He was eventually fatally wounded in his heel by an arrow at the battle of Troy.

We still use the expression 'Achilles heel' in everyday language to mean a person's weakness or vulnerability. Medically we speak of the Achilles tendon as a landmark rather than a weak point.

Achilles tendon injury in ballet dancers

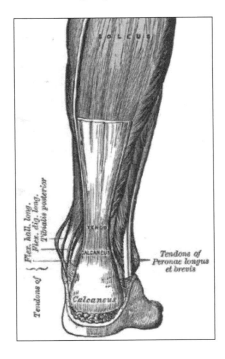

Ballet dancers are prone to several foot injuries, mainly because of the repeated holding of poses on the tips of the toes 'en pointe' position or on the balls of the feet in 'demi-pointe' . Added to this is the fact that dancers tend to spend long hours in rehearsal which can cause over-use injuries. Over-use injuries may be:

1. impingement syndromes of the ankle which limit movement

2. tendon abnormalities - thickening of the tendons at the back of the foot, 9% of these injuries in ballet dancers relate to the Achilles tendon

3. osseous pathology or swelling of the bone marrow

4. ligament abnormalities - these are the most common injuries to ballet dancers

Achilles tendon

These are not uncommon in ballet dancers accounting for 9% of ballet injuries. Tendonitis, paratendonitis and retrocalcaneal bursitis are all encountered.

acromion

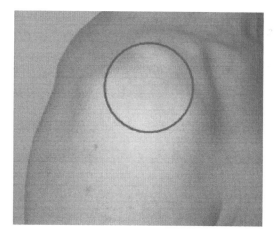

The acromion is also called the 'shoulder tip'. It comes from the Ancient Greek word 'akron' which means tip or extremity and 'omos', the Greek word for 'shoulder'.

The Greek word 'akron' can be seen in the word 'Acropolis' , the famous icon which was built on a summit in Athens.

The prefix 'acro-' also comes from 'akron'. When combined with the suffix -megaly (big) it forms the term describing the condition 'acromegaly' or 'large extremities'

Rotator Cuff Repair

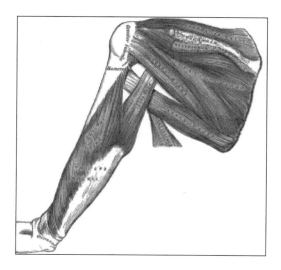

Shoulder injuries are sometimes suffered as a result of sporting accidents. The surgical repair is called Rotator Cuff Repair. The extent of the surgery depends on the severity of the tear in the muscle. There are several muscles which attach to the humerus bone to give full range of movement of the shoulder and arm. Any tear to the muscle causes unrelenting pain and restriction of movement.

If the tear is not repaired, a 'frozen shoulder' is a possible result. In this case, the range of movement is severely limited and this has a flow on effect in many other aspects of a person's life. Dressing and toileting (wiping oneself after toilet use) is more difficult. Pain may still be present leading to a reliance on pain killers.

Surgical repair of a rotator cuff injury may be:

1. Debridement - the trimming and smoothing of a partial tear

2. Reattachment of the tendon to the humerus . In a complete tear the two parts of the thickest part of the tendon is stitched together.

Surgery can be performed as a laparoscopic procedure which results in the patient having three small incisions which are sutured with a single suture each. These are covered with a water-proof dressing so the patient can shower the day after surgery. Recovery tends to be quicker as well as the incisions are very small. This type of surgery is called 'Minimally Invasive Surgery'.

Alternatively, the older surgical option of open surgery is used. This is usually because the tear is very long (at least a few centimetres in length) or if the tear is complex. The incision is therefore a few centimetres in length and is sutured. Recovery time is longer and post-op pain experienced is often more intense.

The follow-up physiotherapy of either methods of Rotator Cuff Repair is very important so that patients regain complete range of movement of their shoulder. Physios teach pendulum exercises where patients swing their arm gently like the pendulum of a clock. Initially ,however, the shoulder is immobilised in a 'collar and cuff' sling until physiotherapy can start a more vigorous exercise programme . Patients are encouraged to do gentle exercises to maintain strength in the muscles until the exercise programme can begin.

amygdala

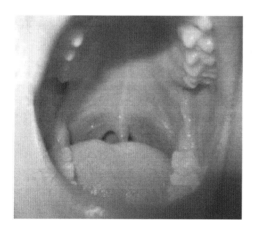

The Greek word 'amygdale' means 'almond' and was borrowed by the Romans and used as 'amygdala' . It is used to describe the tonsil because the tonsil has the shape of an almond. The grey matter in the anterior portion of the temporal lobe which is involved in processing emotions is also called the 'amygdala' because of its almond shape. The corpus amygdaloideum (amygdala found in the brain) are thought to play a part in binge drinking.

The Ancient Greeks and Romans often named parts of the anatomy after objects with the same shape.

artery

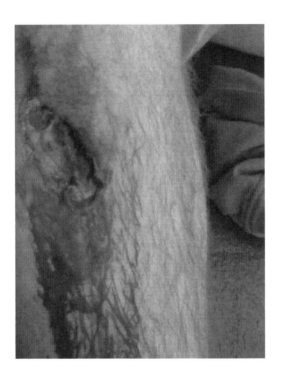

•

The word 'artery' probably derives from the Ancient Greek words 'aer' meaning 'air' and 'terein' meaning 'to keep'. The reason for this is because the Greeks believed that the arteries were windpipes which carried air around the body. The Romans adopted the word into Latin as 'arteria' and continued the belief that arteries carried air around the body.

This belief was only challenged by William Harvey in 1628 when he published his treatise 'Exercitatio Anatomica de Motu Cordis et Sanguinis'.

Link List for medical Etymology

- **Anatomy Clip Art** www.squidoo.com/anatomy-clip-art/157039738

  This is a collection of unusual posters relating to the body - not the usual clip art I was expecting. Suggested art is from All Posters in the main

Learn About The Human Body www.squidoo.com/humans

- comprehensive review from tongue to toe. A mix of medical terminology and children's colouring book suggestions

Medical Etymology: The Origins of Our Language

www.clinicalcorrelations.org/?p=5329

- Interesting article on the surprise discovery of coumarin by a farmer in a clover field which lead to the development of warfarin

Activity 3: In groups, look at the following exercises and discuss the language students will practise during these activities.

Asthma Crossword

Across
1. plastic container used to store asthma medication
3. difficult breathing pattern characterised by noisy sounds on inspiration
4. measures the fastest rate of air that can be exhaled in three readings
7. respiratory disease characterised by wheezing
8. device which administers medication in the form of a fine mist
Down
2. medication which helps to widen the airways
5. device which dispenses asthma medication as an aerosol
6. receptacle for liquid medication in a nebuliser mask

Asthma crossword:

Language practised

Teacher preparation. Looking at the crossword,

1. Which clues would you have difficulty with?

2. How would you prepare yourself for the lesson?

print

save as pdf

Migraine

Instructions: Fill in the gaps below with the modal verbs available in the box.

can	will	can	may	can	have to	can
might	should					

Trigger Factors For Migraine: Environmental factors: A build up of tiredness over the working week _____ increase the risk of a migraine attack. Other factors like emotion, stress and missed meals (hypoglycaemia) _____ also play a part. In addition, cigarette smoke and strong odours (e.g. perfume or paint) _____ bring on a strong headache or migraine. Hormonal changes: Hormone replacement therapy (HRT), oral contraceptives or pregnancy _____ be triggers of migraine. Food or ingredients: Some people _____ react to certain foods like pickles or cured meats as they increase the incidence of migraine. Chemicals like monosodium glutamate, sulphites and artificial sweeteners _____ be avoided too as they _____ trigger headaches. Some people also _____ stop drinking alcohol, caffeine and chocolate because they _____ often make migraines more frequent.

9 modal verbs to fit

Name: _____

Mark: _____ / _____

Back to generate Answersheet

Activity 4: You take a photo of your son/daughter/partner/friend who gives permission for the use of the photo. How might you use the photo in an EMP course?

For example, the following photos are of my son and daughter who have given permission for the use of the photos.

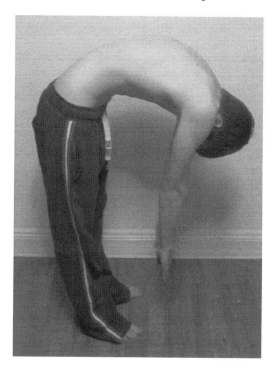 

Suggested use of the photos:

1.

2.

3.

4.

Authorsden article: Using health-related articles to produce teaching resources

by Virginia Allum

I like to create as many teaching resources as I can, using online health articles as a basis. I have written an article about Rabies as an example of a lesson I would use in a Medical English classroom. The article gives students the opportunity to:

1. Read and discuss a health article which is of current interest – the incident referred to happened this year.

2. Review some prefixes and suffixes and medical terms. For example,

trans-

lyssa-

encephalo-

-itis

hydro-

-phobia

dys-

-phagia

3. Review the peripheral and central nervous system – perhaps leading to presentations or flow on activities which students can make themselves for the class (crosswords, closes and matching activities)

4. Review terms relating to disease and treatment, for example,

case

treated at ..hospital

viral infection, infected by

transmitted

disease

incubation

symptoms

malaise

vaccination, vaccine

prophylaxis

5. Identify compound words in the text –ask students to comment on the forms of the compound words (some have a space between the two words, some a hyphen and some are written together)

viral infection

bat-handler

hotspot

6. Discuss the difference between 'hydrophobia' (irrational fear of drinking water and other liquids) and 'aqua phobia' (irrational fear of getting into water e.g. the ocean)

Preparation for the lesson. Produce a worksheet which practises some or all of the suggestions above (prefixes, compound words, words relating to medicine). Also include 3 – 4 comprehension questions.

Before you start, ask students what they already know about rabies. Start a mind map and add to it as students learn more about the disease.

Ask students to read the article and complete the worksheet.

An extension exercise: World Rabies Day is September 28. Ask students to research the day and report on the events occurring in their country (or a country they select)

What is Rabies?

BBC Health News (www.bbc.co.uk/news/uk-england-london-18182734) confirmed a rabies case in London on 24 May 2012.

A patient who was bitten by a dog in South East Asia before arriving in the UK has a confirmed case of rabies. The patient was treated at London's Hospital for Tropical Diseases but, unfortunately, died a few days after arrival.

Rabies is a viral infection which is transmitted to humans via the saliva of animals, most often dogs (99% of all cases).The word rabies comes from the Latin word rabies meaning 'rage'.

Bats in Northern Europe can be infected by a rabies-like virus called European Bat Lyssavirus (EBLV). A case of infection via a bat was recorded in a bat-handler in Scotland in 2003 but it is otherwise unknown in the UK.

The word lyssa' is the Greek word for 'rabies' and refers to a structure on the tip of the dog's tongue. This used to be thought to be the cause of rabies. These days, lyssa is only used in the term lyssavirus meaning a 'rabies-like virus'.

Globally, more than 55,000 people die from rabies each year. The hotspots are Asia (around 31,000 cases) and Africa (around 24,000 cases). India has the most cases of any country because of the large numbers of stray dogs.

As far as Europe is concerned, the following countries are considered rabies-free Austria, UK, Ireland, Belgium, Holland, Luxembourg, France, Switzerland, Germany (since 2008) , Portugal, Spain, Italy, Greece, Malta, Denmark, Norway, Sweden, Finland and Iceland.

Rabies has still been reported in most of the 19 countries of Central and Eastern Europe. The main vectors or sources of the disease are the red fox (Vulpes vulpes) ,the raccoon dog (Nyctereutes procyonoides) and cats (reported in the Ukraine). Croatia and Serbia are the two countries in Eastern Europe where no human rabies cases have been reported for over 30 years.

The disease is unheard of in Australia and New Zealand, however, the Australian Bat Lyssavirus (ABLV) which infects the native Australian bat is similar to rabies.

Rabies is a viral infection which eventually causes encephalitis. The long incubation period of a few months relates to the time the virus takes to travel from the peripheral nervous system to the central nervous system.

Early symptoms include malaise, headache and fever. If the disease is not identified the patient will experience acute pain, violent jerky movements and hydrophobia. Hydrophobia causes patients to have dysphagia (difficulty swallowing) , panic when presented with something to drink and an inability to quench their thirst. In the final stages, patients may exhibit manic behaviour but eventually become extremely lethargic and then become comatose and die.

There are three modes of treatment depending on the stage of the disease.

1. Prevention: vaccination with three injections over a month.

2.Post-exposure prophylaxis – This is the treatment started after a dog bite to prevent infection with the rabies virus. The wound is cleaned and an injection of rabies immunoglobulin (antibodies) is given to the patient. Finally, a course of the rabies vaccine.

3. Supportive or Palliative Care – This is the only treatment available for an advanced case of rabies infection. Patients are kept as comfortable as possible.

Session 1: Needs Analysis

Needs analysis is an important aspect to be considered when designing any ESP course. This session will look at the differing needs of learners, with a particular focus on the requirements of pre-experience and in-work learners. It will look at methods of information gathering before pre-course and in-course analysis, and will discuss how this information can be used most effectively. Typical problems which can arise when carrying out needs analyses in a practical setting will also be outlined, along with possible approaches to overcome these.

Session 1: Developing a needs analysis

Why are you studying EMP?

- ○ to be able to work in healthcare in an English-speaking country?

- ○ to be able to communicate with English-speaking patients in your own country?

- ○ to be able to read academic articles about medicine or other healthcare topics?

- ○ to be able to present a paper at an international conference

- ○ to be able to teach EMP?

- ○ Other

Why an EMP course?

Keep the following in mind...

1. To be workplace-ready in an English-speaking country

- Specialised vocabulary used by nurses

- Need for accuracy in communication (safety)

- General English courses are not appropriate – limited use in healthcare environment

- Healthcare environment can be pressured – need for confidence which comes from rehearsal and practice

- need to include regional vocabulary where practicable – also focus on speciality treatments or surgery

2. To communicate in a healthcare environment using English as a common language

- All the above

- may be focussed on particular areas e.g A&E

- Medical Tourism

3. Compulsory part of a nursing or medical degree

- French Nursing course – focus on ultimate need to critique a health topic

- forthcoming inclusion in Italian medical and nursing degrees in 2014-5

4. Desire to participate in conferences and writing of academic articles.

- Brazilian nurses want to be active participants in conferences instead of receiving information via translation

- increasing global standards in nursing and medicine –Best Practice

5. Preparation for language competence testing before registration to practice

- currently in UK, non-EU health care workers are tested

- changes in progress for all workers, EU and non-EU workers to be tested.

- current 'Responsible Officers' who monitor the language competence of overseas doctors

6. New regulations – Responsible Officers and overseas doctors

Responsible Officers blog

www. englishfornursingandhealthcare.com

On 17 May, 2012, The NHS employers website published an article called 'Consultation on responsible officer regulations' advising that surveys for public opinion on the amendments to regulations relating to Responsible Officers (RO) are to be submitted to the Department of Health by 13 July 2012. According to the website, consultation by the Department of Health will be in three areas, namely:

1. Deciding on the role of the NHS Commissioning Board in nominating and appointing Responsible Officers

2. Deciding on the role of Responsible Officers in assessing the language competence of overseas-trained doctors who are working in England.

3. Establishing whether a local authority will come within the definition of 'designated bodies' if the local authority has a connection to a public health doctor for example and whether a local authority could act as a responsible officer for doctors.

As an EMP (English for Medical Purposes) specialist, my main interest is in the area of language competency assessment of overseas trained doctors. The background to this issue is the fact that currently in the UK only non-EU healthcare professionals (doctors, nurses, physiotherapists, dentists etc) have their language skills assessed. I am a non-EU nurse who had to pass each of the four skills of an IELTS (International English Language Testing System) at a minimum of 7.0 before registering as a nurse in the UK. English is my first language. The UK is unusual in comparison with other English-speaking countries in that only non-EU workers are tested: EU health care professionals do not have their English language skills tested before working in the UK.

Recently, this anomaly was reviewed at European Parliament level which then started the process of thinking of the testing of all overseas-trained doctors but not all overseas-trained nurses for various, to my mind, bizarre reasons. Leaving this aside, I was interested to read Chapter Three of the 'Consultation document: Responsible officers in the new health architecture'

Looking through the chapter, I came across a few points which raised questions in my mind about the effectiveness of the current system and likely effectiveness of the mooted system. First, I read that the The National Health Service (Performers Lists) Regulations 2004 already require Primary Care Trusts (PCTs) to refuse to admit overseas-trained doctors, dentists or opticians to a Performers List if the PCT does not feel that the applicant 'has the appropriate English language knowledge to enable them to carry out their function as a doctor in the PCT's area.' The idea being that the The Performers List ensures that the overseas doctor is 'fit for practice' i.e can work safely by being able to communicate effectively in English and therefore safe patient care is ensured.

Responsible officers in England (other countries in the UK have different regulations) have the same or similar functions to the PCTs . However, whilst ROs have a duty to check that medical practitioners have the required qualifications and experience for the job, there is no specific duty to check language competency.

On the other hand, The Coalition programme for government committed to ensure that foreign 'healthcare professionals' (did this include nurses?) have an adequate level of language competence so that NHS patients are not put at risk or harmed because of communication break downs.

Looking at the situation of doctors (as the nurses' situation hangs in the balance) ,The Coalition agreement would tend to suggest that the RO legislation needs to be amended to make it clear that the function of a Responsible Officer explicitly extends to the testing of language competency before an overseas-trained doctor can set foot in a hospital and communicate with patients and colleagues. My first thought was, ' How is this to be done?' The following section (section 3.7) talks about assessing language in a 'proportionate way' including a 'proportionate use of language tests'. My next thought was ,' Which language tests are they thinking of ? This is not explained or mentioned from what I can see.
The only reference to 'how this competence would be assessed' seems to be in stating that guidance would be sought from the GMC and the NHS Commissioning Board. 'Guidance could also be amended quickly to take account of changing circumstances, such as any scheme intended to apply across healthcare professionals more generally'. I presumed this to refer to nursing.

Again, the proposal that ROs will notify concerns regarding language competency to the GMC does not include any clues about how the RO will assess language competency.
Cost was also alluded to but felt to be quite low, as 'Under the existing system PCTs and NHS Trusts are required to undertake checks' so it was felt there would be no change in test costs. But, I still felt I was missing something. What tests? My understanding was that there is no testing of EU doctors allowed so how can there be existing costs for 'checks' or are

these 'checks' informal conversations with prospective doctors which are costed as admin time?

My final musings were about the ROs and their own competence to assess language competency. Surely this should be done by language specialists? If not, why did I have to undertake an IELTS test (a language test administered by language specialists) before I was able to apply for nursing registration in the UK? It is already a silly situation whereby doctors and nurses (and other health care practitioners) from English-speaking countries who most probably count English as their first language have to front up for an IELTS test when their European colleagues who probably do not count English as their first language, do not. Having said that, in most English-speaking countries, everyone fronts up to prove their language competency before registering as a doctor or nurse or similar.

In Canada, nurses sit a CELBAN (Canadian English Language Benchmark Assessment for Nurses) http://www.celban.org/celban/display_page.asp?page_id=1 which specifically tests the ability to speak the English required for the healthcare environment . In other words, EMP. The question of whether IELTS is an appropriate language test for healthcare workers is another issue, however, at least it is a language test of some sort and of international recognition.

Many NHS hospitals have English classes for overseas doctors and nurses already working in the system. Obviously the need is recognized but it would seem a little like closing the stable door a bit too late.

What do stakeholders demand of overseas nurses?

- **Ability to communicate effectively**
- Safe practice
- High standards of technical knowledge
- Cultural sensitivity and awareness
- Good teamwork
- Ability to work with other Health Care Professionals

Possible further changes in need analysis for EMP

- Specific language testing for medical professionals - currently OET only → test prep materials
- IELTS more often used – not medical focus
- Use of a specific medical test → need for test prep materials

Session 2: Methodology

This session discusses the benefits of integrating as far as possible a methodology employed in the training of L1 medical practitioners; one which maximises use of authentic texts and tasks and allows learners to concentrate on the development of communicative competencies in their particular context. Participants will be provided with suitable frameworks for use in their own context, e.g. the Calgary-Cambridge Observation Guide.

What is the Calgary-Cambridge Observation Guide?

https://www.gpnotebook.co.uk/simplepage.cfm?ID=-932511677

The five tasks of the consultation are:

A. Initiating the session

B. Gathering information

C. Building the relationship

D. Giving information - explaining and planning

E. Closing the session

The expanded framework goes into the five tasks in greater detail.

Reference:

SM Kurtz and JD Silverman: The Calgary-Cambridge Referenced Observation Guides: an aid to defining the curriculum and organising teaching in communication training programmes Medical Education 1996 (30) 83-9.

CALGARY - CAMBRIDGE GUIDE TO THE MEDICAL INTERVIEW –

COMMUNICATION PROCESS

INITIATING THE SESSION

Establishing initial rapport

1. Greets patient and obtains patient's name

2. Introduces self, role and nature of interview; obtains consent if necessary

3. Demonstrates respect and interest, attends to patient's physical comfort

Identifying the reason(s) for the consultation

4. Identifies the patient's problems or the issues that the patient wishes to address with appropriate opening question (e.g. "What problems brought you to the hospital?" or "What would you like to discuss today?" or "What questions did you hope to get answered today?")

5. Listens attentively to the patient's opening statement, without interrupting or directing patient's response

6. Confirms list and screens for further problems (e.g. "so that's headaches and tiredness; anything else……?")

7. Negotiates agenda taking both patient's and physician's needs into account

GATHERING INFORMATION

Exploration of patient's problems

8. Encourages patient to tell the story of the problem(s) from when first started to the present in own words (clarifying reason for presenting now)

9. Uses open and closed questioning technique, appropriately moving from open to closed

10. Listens attentively, allowing patient to complete statements without interruption and leaving space for patient to think before answering or go on after pausing

11. Facilitates patient's responses verbally and non–verbally e.g. use of encouragement, silence, repetition, paraphrasing, interpretation

12. Picks up verbal and non–verbal cues (body language, speech, facial

expression, affect); checks out and acknowledges as appropriate

13.Clarifies patient's statements that are unclear or need amplification (e.g. "Could you explain what you mean by light headed")

14. Periodically summarises to verify own understanding of what the patient has said; invites patient to correct interpretation or provide further information.

15. Uses concise, easily understood questions and comments, avoids or adequately explains jargon

16. Establishes dates and sequence of events

Additional skills for understanding the patient's perspective

17. Actively determines and appropriately explores:

- patient's ideas (i.e. beliefs re cause)

- patient's concerns (i.e. worries) regarding each problem

- patient's expectations (i.e., goals, what help the patient had expected for each problem)

- effects: how each problem affects the patient's life

18. Encourages patient to express feelings

PROVIDING STRUCTURE

Making organisation overt

19. Summarises at the end of a specific line of inquiry to confirm understanding before moving on to the next section

20. Progresses from one section to another using signposting, transitional statements; includes rationale for next section

Attending to flow

21. Structures interview in logical sequence

22. Attends to timing and keeping interview on task

BUILDING RELATIONSHIP

Using appropriate non-verbal behaviour

23. Demonstrates appropriate non–verbal behaviour

- eye contact, facial expression

- posture, position & movement

- vocal cues e.g. rate, volume, tone

24. If reads, writes notes or uses computer, does in a manner that does not interfere with dialogue or rapport

25. Demonstrates appropriate confidence

Developing rapport

26. Accepts legitimacy of patient's views and feelings; is not judgmental

27. Uses empathy to communicate understanding and appreciation of the patient's feelings or predicament; overtly acknowledges patient's views and feelings

28. Provides support: expresses concern, understanding, willingness to help; acknowledges coping efforts and appropriate self care; offers partnership

29. Deals sensitively with embarrassing and disturbing topics and physical pain, including when associated with physical examination

Involving the patient

30. Shares thinking with patient to encourage patient's involvement (e.g. "What I'm thinking now is....")

31. Explains rationale for questions or parts of physical examination that could appear to be non-sequiturs

32. During physical examination, explains process, asks permission

EXPLANATION AND PLANNING

Providing the correct amount and type of information

33. Chunks and checks: gives information in manageable chunks, checks for understanding, uses patient's response as a guide to how to proceed

34. Assesses patient's starting point: asks for patient's prior knowledge early on when giving information, discovers extent of patient's wish for information

35. Asks patients what other information would be helpful e.g. aetiology, prognosis

36. Gives explanation at appropriate times: avoids giving advice, information or reassurance prematurely

Aiding accurate recall and understanding

37. Organises explanation: divides into discrete sections, develops a logical sequence

38. Uses explicit categorisation or signposting (e.g. "There are three important things that I would like to discuss. 1st..." "Now, shall we move on to.")

39. Uses repetition and summarising to reinforce information

40. Uses concise, easily understood language, avoids or explains jargon

41. Uses visual methods of conveying information: diagrams, models, written information and instructions

42. Checks patient's understanding of information given (or plans made): e.g. by

asking patient to restate in own words; clarifies as necessary

Achieving a shared understanding: incorporating the patient's perspective

43. Relates explanations to patient's illness framework: to previously elicited ideas, concerns and expectations

44. Provides opportunities and encourages patient to contribute: to ask questions, seek clarification or express doubts; responds appropriately

45. Picks up verbal and non-verbal cues e.g. patient's need to contribute information or ask questions, information overload, distress

46. Elicits patient's beliefs, reactions and feelings re information given, terms used; acknowledges and addresses where necessary

Planning: shared decision making

47. Shares own thinking as appropriate: ideas, thought processes, dilemmas

48. Involves patient by making suggestions rather than directives

49. Encourages patient to contribute their thoughts: ideas, suggestions and preferences

50. Negotiates a mutually acceptable plan

51. Offers choices: encourages patient to make choices and decisions to the level that they wish

52. Checks with patient if accepts plans, if concerns have been addressed

CLOSING THE SESSION

Forward planning

53. Contracts with patient re next steps for patient and physician

54. Safety nets, explaining possible unexpected outcomes, what to do if plan is not working, when and how to seek help

Ensuring appropriate point of closure

55. Summarises session briefly and clarifies plan of care

56. Final check that patient agrees and is comfortable with plan and asks if any corrections, questions or other items to discuss

OPTIONS IN EXPLANATION AND PLANNING (includes content)

IF discussing investigations and procedures

57. Provides clear information on procedures, eg, what patient might experience, how patient will be informed of results

58. Relates procedures to treatment plan: value, purpose

59. Encourages questions about and discussion of potential anxieties or negative

outcomes

IF discussing opinion and significance of problem

60. Offers opinion of what is going on and names if possible

61. Reveals rationale for opinion

62. Explains causation, seriousness, expected outcome, short and long term consequences

63. Elicits patient's beliefs, reactions, concerns re opinion

IF negotiating mutual plan of action

64. Discusses options eg, no action, investigation, medication or surgery, non-drug treatments (physiotherapy, walking aides, fluids, counselling, preventive measures)

65. Provides information on action or treatment offered

name , steps involved, how it works , benefits and advantages, possible side effects

66. Obtains patient's view of need for action, perceived benefits, barriers, motivation

67. Accepts patient's views, advocates alternative viewpoint as necessary

68. Elicits patient's reactions and concerns about plans and treatments including acceptability

69. Takes patient's lifestyle, beliefs, cultural background and abilities into consideration

70. Encourages patient to be involved in implementing plans, to take responsibility and be self-reliant

71. Asks about patient support systems, discusses other support available

References:

Kurtz SM, Silverman JD, Draper J (1998) Teaching and Learning Communication Skills in Medicine. Radcliffe Medical Press (Oxford)

Silverman JD, Kurtz SM, Draper J (1998) Skills for Communicating with Patients. Radcliffe Medical Press (Oxford)

Session 3: Authentic Materials I: Introduction

This session will focus on how to exploit authentic materials effectively. After a brief discussion about the meaning of 'authentic', we will look at the advantages and disadvantages of authentic materials within the context of medical and nursing English, and look at some examples from existing courses. Issues of Data Protection when using authentic materials will also be considered.

Examples of 'near authentic' materials from

'Cambridge English for Nursing' books and 'English for Medical Purposes' books

- handover sheets

- charts

- hospital documents

Near authentic documents from 'English for Medical Purposes: Spelling and Vocabulary'

http://www.lulu.com/shop/virginia-allum/english-for-medical-purposes-spelling-and-vocabulary/paperback/product-20231530.html

SBAR

- Used as a template for reporting changes in patient condition

- Language used to explain the nature of a hospital event and the assessments which have been done.

SBAR REPORTING

BEFORE CALLING:
1. Assess the patient
2. Know the admission diagnosis
3. Read most recent events / progress
4. Have available: **Observation Chart, Fluid Balance Chart, Drug Chart, Latest Laboratory Results, DNR Status**
5. Be sure you are calling appropriate team / physician

WARD: _____

DATE: _____

TIME OF CALL: _____

REPORTING NURSE: _____

PERSON CONTACTED: _____

TIME PATIENT REVIEWED: _____

SITUATION

State your name and area of work
"I am calling about ...." (Give patient name and location)
"The situation is ...." (Briefly outline the problem)

What it is
When it started
How severe
MEWS score

BACKGROUND

"The background is ...."

State admission diagnosis and date of admission
Give brief, relevant medical history and treatment to date

ASSESSMENT

"My assessment is ...."
List changes in the patient's condition, which give cause for concern:
AIRWAY e.g. Is the airway patent? Noisy breathing? Is the patient receiving OXYGEN?
BREATHING e.g. Respiratory rate, breathing pattern, SpO2, skin colour,
CIRCULATION e.g. Pulse rate, rhythm changes, blood pressure, CRT
DISABILITY e.g. AVPU assessment, change in GCS, pain assessment, blood glucose
EXPOSURE e.g. wound drainage, urine output
State here if you are concerned that the patient is rapidly deteriorating and at risk of cardiac arrest

RECOMMENDATION

"I recommend that you ...... / I would like you to ...."
State what you would like to see done e.g. Come to assess the patient immediately,
Review DNR status; consider transferring the patient to Critical Care
"How long will you be?" (Ensure you are given a time for the patient to be assessed)
"Is there anything specific you would like me to do now?"
E.g. CXR, ABG, ECG, Contact Outreach Team

SBAR REPORTING

State your name and area of work

"I am calling about ……." (Give patient name and location) What it is

"The situation is ………" (Briefly outline the problem) When it started

How severe

MEWS score

SITUATION

"The background is ………….."

State admission diagnosis and date of admission

Give brief, relevant medical history and treatment to date

BACKGROUND

"My assessment is …………………"

List changes in the patient's condition, which give cause for concern:

AIRWAY e.g. Is the airway patent? Noisy breathing? Is the patient receiving OXYGEN?

BREATHING e.g. Respiratory rate, breathing pattern, SpO2, skin colour,

CIRCULATION e.g. Pulse rate, rhythm changes, blood pressure, CRT

DISABILITY e.g. AVPU assessment, change in GCS, pain assessment, blood glucose

EXPOSURE e.g. wound drainage, urine output

State here if you are concerned that the patient is rapidly deteriorating and at risk of cardiac arrest

ASSESSMENT

"I recommend that you …… / I would like you to ……….."

State what you would like to see done e.g. Come to assess the patient immediately,

Review DNR status; consider transferring the patient to Critical Care

"How long will you be?" (Ensure you are given a time for the patient to be assessed)

"Is there anything specific you would like me to do now?"

E.g. CXR, ABG, ECG, Contact Outreach Team

SAGO - Standard Adult General Observation

http://nswhealth.moodle.com.au/DOH/DETECT/content/00_worry/when_to_worry_07.htm

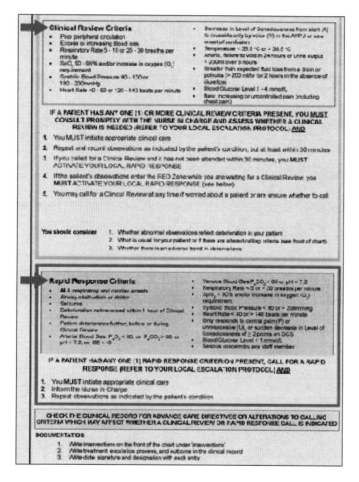

http://nswhealth.moodle.com.au/DOH/DETECT/content/00_worry/applets/Adult_Observation_Chart4.html

DETECT Manual

Chap 1: When to worry (pdf 765kB)

Chap 2: I can't breathe (pdf 766kB)

Chap 3: Warm hands, warm feet (pdf 427kB)

Chap 4: The five causes of anuria (.pdf 335kB)

Chap 5: The confused patient (.pdf 257kB)

Date																			
Time																			

B L O O D
P R E S S U R E

40 — 260
— 250
39 — 240
— 230
38 — 220
37.5 — 210
37 — 200
— 190
36 — 180
— 170
35 — 160
— 150
34 — 140
— 130
33 — 120
— 110
— 100
P U L S E — 90
— 80
— 70
— 60
— 50
— 40
— 30

CNS	
Resp. Rate	
O2 Saturation	
O2 Delivered % / Litres	
EWS Score	
PCAS / total Epidural rate	
Pain Score	
Nausea Score	
BM	

Date										
Time										

260 — 40
250
240 — 39
230
220 — 38
210 — 37.5
200 — 37
190
180 — 36
170
160 — 35
150
140 — 34
130
120 — 33
110
100
90
80
70
60
50
40
30

CNS	
Resp. Rate	
O2 Saturation	
O2 Delivered % / Litres	
EWS Score	
PCAS / total Epidural rate	
Pain Score	
Nausea Score	
BM	

| Age. | | Hosp No: | |

The Adult Early Warning Scoring System

Score	0	1	2	3
Heart rate	51 - 100	41 - 50 / 101 - 110	< 40 / 111 - 130	>130
Systolic BP	101 - 160	81 - 100 / 161 - 200	71 - 80 / > 200	<70
Resp. Rate	9 -14	15 - 20	< 8 / 21 - 29	>30
Temp.	36.5 - 37.5	35.1 - 36.0 / > 37.5	< 35	
CNS Response	Awake	To Voice	To Pain	Unconscious

SEEK SENIOR HELP IMMEDIATELY IF THE PATIENT SCORES 3 OR MORE ON E.W.S.

Time Dr. Informed: Date:

Initials:

Pt's usual BP: Pulse:

SEEK SENIOR HELP IMMEDIATELY IF THE OXYGEN SATURATION IS LESS THAN 90% ON AIR, OR LESS THAN 95% ON OXYGEN

Pain assessment tool: *on movement

0   10
No Pain   Worst pain

Nausea score
0 = No symptoms   2 = Retching
1 = Nauseated   3 = Vomiting
           S = Sleeping

Urinalysis: Blood Glucose:

Observation Chart

Recent article on BBC News. July 2012

Before you start, review these terms,

Vital Signs	Blood Pressure, Temperature, Pulse and Respirations – all signs which are vital or essential for life
Early Warning Score (EWS)	this score is a result of the review of blood pressure reading, temperature, pulse and respirations. Scoring below a certain number indicates that the patient may be starting to have difficulties
bedside chart	patient information which is kept at the foot of the bed. Nurses complete the information as they do the procedure e.g taking a temperature, taking a blood glucose level
respiratory rate (RR)	how many breaths per minute a patient takes
level of consciousness (LOC)	how alert a patient is e.g alert and oriented, drowsy and unresponsive, comatose
critical care	Also called Intensive Care Unit (ICU) or Intensive Therapy Unit (ITU). Unit in the hospital where patients are monitored closely by one nurse who stays by the bedside all the time
ad hoc	Latin expression meaning 'improvised or not for a specific purpose'

BBC NEWS

27 July 2012 Last updated at 01:08

Call for national system for monitoring vital signs

By Nick Triggle Health correspondent, BBC News

The way **vital signs** such as blood pressure and temperature are monitored in hospitals needs to be standardised across the NHS, experts say.

Currently over 100 different models are used, causing confusion and sometimes delays in patients getting help.

A joint group of senior doctors and nurses said moving to a national system would save thousands of lives a year.

The group, with the backing of NHS leaders, has put forward a system it wants adopted in the UK within a year.

The scheme - called the National **Early Warning Score** - has been drawn up by the royal colleges of physicians and nursing after reviewing many of the **bedside chart** models being used across the NHS.

It is based on a scoring system for six measures - **respiratory rate**, oxygen levels, temperature, blood pressure, pulse rate and **level of consciousness**.

The chart, which is also colour coded, is then used to determine if a patient needs further assessment and potentially admitting to **critical care**.

The royal colleges said it could halve the number of avoidable deaths in hospitals, which would mean about 6,000 lives a year being saved.

Prof Bryan Williams, chair of the working party which drew up the new system, said it would mean that as staff move around the health service they would not need training and help getting used to new ways of working.

He added: "It has the potential to transform patient safety in our hospitals and improve outcomes, it is hugely important."

While it is not compulsory that hospitals adopt the system, Prof Williams said as it had the backing of the two royal colleges as well as the Department of Health he hoped the NHS would embrace it over the next 12 months.

He also wants to see it used outside hospitals, for example when GPs and ambulance crews are assessing whether patients need to be transferred to hospital.

The system will not apply to the care of pregnant women and children under 16.

Prof Sir Bruce Keogh, the medical director of the NHS in England, gave the initiative his backing, saying catching deterioration in the early stages would lead to "huge improvements".

Katherine Murphy, chief executive of the Patients Association, said the national system should be introduced "urgently".

"The public will be shocked to learn that the NHS has been operating such an **ad hoc** system.

"It is therefore no surprise that the experience and outcome for so many patients is a negative one."

Activity 5:   Small group discussion

Imagine you are a group of EMP students. In groups of 4, discuss why doctors and nurses are suggesting adoption of the new system. What language would you expect to come out of this exercise?

Suggestions:

It will make it easier for…

It may improve patient…….

The colour code will…

WATERLOW PRESSURE ULCER RISK ASSESSMENT TOOL

Add totals to obtain risk score. Several scores per category can be calculated.

Has the patient previously had a pressure ulcer?   **Yes**   **No**

SEX/AGE		BUILD/WEIGHT FOR HEIGHT		SPECIAL RISKS	
		BMI		**TISSUE MALNUTRITION**	
Male	1				
Female	2	Average (20 – 24.9)	0	Terminal cachexia	8
14-49	1	Above average (25 – 29.9)	1	Multiple organ failure	8
50-64	2	Obese > 30	2	Single organ failure ie.	5
65-74	3	Below average < 20	3	(resp. renal, cardiac & liver)	
75-80	4			Peripheral vascular disease	5
81+	5	BMI = WT (Kg)		Anaemia (Hb<8)	2
		HT (m²)		Smoking	1
MOBILITY		**CONTINENCE**		**NEUROLOGICAL DEFICIT**	
Fully	0	Complete/catheterised	0	Diabetes, MS, CVA,	4 - 6
Restless/fidgety	1	Urine incontinence	1	Motor/sensory paraplegia	
Apathetic	2	Faecal incontinence	2	(maximum of 6)	
Restricted	3	Urinary and faecal	3	**MAJOR SURGERY OR TRAUMA**	
Bedbound	4	incontinence		Orthopaedic/Spinal	5
(eg. traction)				On table > 2hrs (past 48hrs)	5
Chairbound	5			> 6hrs (past 48hrs)	8
(eg. wheelchair)					
NUTRITIONAL STATUS		**SKIN TYPE VISUAL RISK AREAS**		**MEDICATION**	
Nutritional score from Malnutrition screening tool below		Healthy	0	Cytotoxics	
		Tissue paper	1	Steroids	4
		Dry	1	Anti-inflammatory	
		Oedematous	1		
		Clammy, pyrexia	1	(maximum of 4)	
		Discoloured Stage 1	2		
		Pressure ulcer Stage 2-4	3		

Abbreviations	Meaning
BMI	Body Mass Index
WT	weight
HT	height
kg	kilogram
m²	square metres
Hb	haemoglobin
resp.	respiratory
MS	multiple sclerosis
CVA	cerebrovascular accident. Also called CVE cerebrovascular event

Falls Risk

FALL RISK STATUS: *(Circle)*: LOW / MEDIUM / HIGH ➡	**List Fall Status on Care Plan/ Flow Chart**
IMPORTANT: IF **HIGH**, *COMMENCE FALL ALERT*	

PART 2: RISK FACTOR CHECKLIST		Y/N
Vision	Reports / observed difficulty seeing - objects / signs / finding way around	
Mobility	Mobility status unknown or appears unsafe / impulsive / forgets gait aid	
Transfers	Transfer status unknown or appears unsafe ie. over-reaches, impulsive	
Behaviours	Observed or reported agitation, confusion, disorientation	
	Difficulty following instructions or non-compliant (observed or known)	
Activities of Daily Living (A.D.L's)	Observed risk-taking behaviours, or reported from referrer / previous facility	
	Observed unsafe use of equipment	
	Unsafe footwear / inappropriate clothing	
Environment	Difficulties with orientation to environment i.e. areas between bed / bathroom / dining room	
Nutrition	Underweight / low appetite	
Continence	Reported or known urgency / nocturia / accidents	
Other		

falls	any accidental falling over e.g because unsteady on feet
fall alert	means of telling staff to be careful regarding the likelihood of the patient falling
trips	accidental falling over an object in the way of a person
slips	accidental sliding and falling usually related to liquid on the floor
risk (of)	the probability that something may happen
at risk (patient)	a patient who is at risk of something e.g falls
status	classification of the severity of risk e.g low risk status
impulsive	actions taken before careful consideration
gait aid	also called walking aid e.g walking stick
over reach	does not stop at the position which is safe and keeps moving
confusion	confused (adj) exhibits unclear thoughts
disorientation	disoriented (adj) unsure of correct names of people, place or time
inappropriate	something which is not normal for a particular circumstance

MUST

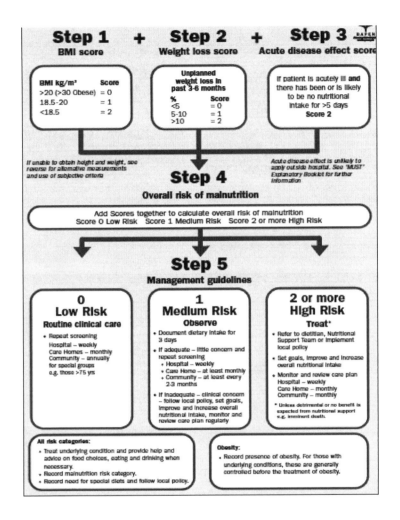

score	a number gained after adding up subsections
screen	tests or procedures used to diagnose a disease or condition
dietary intake	the food and drink a patient eats and drinks
special diet	diet for particular conditions e.g low cholesterol diet
obesity	extreme overweight

Unit from 'English for Medical Purposes: Healthcare Assistants'

http://www.lulu.com/shop/virginia-allum/english-for-medical-purposes-health-care-assistants/paperback/product-20113590.html

Patient Confidentiality

Before you start, review these terms,

patient confidentiality	keeping information about a patient's health information secure
privacy	keeping personal information or parts of the body away from public view
Data Protection	keeping sensitive information secure and available only to those who are allowed to see it
Caldicott principle	general principles which are used before using patient information
protocol	set of written guidelines or rules
guideline	statements which help staff to know the correct way to do a procedure
next-of-kin	a family member or close friend who is contacted in an emergency (kin = family)
breach	old form of 'break' now usually seen in legal documents

Read the following abridged text from the Department of Health site. From

http://www.dh.gov.uk/

Patient Confidentiality Model

The model outlines the requirements that must be met in order to provide patients with a

confidential service. There are four areas which must be covered if patient information can be

said to be held confidentially.

The four are:

PROTECT – look after patient information safely

Staff follow a number of guidelines so that patient information is protected.

- all staff and volunteers are always fully aware of their

  responsibilities regarding patient confidentiality

- patient information is recorded accurately

- patient information is kept away from view

- patient information is stored in a secure place

- patient information is used and disclosed with great care

INFORM – make sure patients know how their information is being used

- check that patients have read and understood patient confidentiality information

  leaflets

- inform patients when information has been recorded in the their patient record e.g if

  patients have a discussion with staff which is recorded so all staff are aware of the

  situation

- make sure that patients know when their information is being disclosed to others e.g

  during a handover

- check that patients are aware of the choices they have with regard to the use of their patient record

- deal with any concerns patients have regarding disclosure of their information

- always respect the rights of patients to make decisions about their health information, especially in situations which are highly sensitive

PROVIDE CHOICE – patients are able to decide   whether their information can be used by anyone else

- ask patients before using their patient information if it is not to be used in direct patient care e.g for research

- respect the decision not to allow the use of their health information

- ensure that patients understand the implications of not allowing the use of their health information

IMPROVE –   look for ways to ensure staff follow best practice procedures for data protection

- establish training or support where staff are uncertain of best practice procedures

- report possible breaches or risk of breaches

Ex 25: Complete the information below about ensuring patient confidentiality. Use the words in the box below

public health	identifying	obligation	accurately	public places	gossiping
confidential					

Keeping patient information _____ is an obligation for all staff and also for any people invited onto the hospital ward e.g external contractors such as electricians and volunteers.

Patient Confidentiality is a duty which is protected by laws such as The Data Protection Act 1998 and The Human Rights Act 1998. Staff also have a professional _____ under their work contract to maintain information safety.

Patient information must be recorded_____. It's important to maintain proper records for good patient care.

It's just as important to keeping patient information private and secure.

Privacy may include:

- not _____about a patient, that is, 'talking behind a person's back'

- respecting confidential information unless it must be handed on for _____ reasons e.g a disclosure of TB

- taking care when discussing cases in _____ e.g discussing a case with a colleague when advice is needed or giving a bedside handover

- not _____ the patient by name unless necessary. Many wards identify only a bed number on a handover sheet so patient information cannot be associated with a particular patient.

Patient information which is written must also be kept secure. Written patient information may be handwritten or electronic e.g email or intranet. This information is protected by:

- logging off so computer screens do not remain open when unattended

- not leaving medical notes or files in areas which are open to public access e.g at the nurse's station.

- keeping all files and portable computers under lock and key when not actually being used.

- shredding information which is no longer needed e.g handover sheets

Ex 26:   Match the terms 1- 6 with their correct meanings a- f

1. confidential	a) information
2. privacy	b) not at risk of being lost or seen by the wrong person
3. data	c) tear paper into very small pieces
4. secure	d) free from intrusion
5. identity	e) private , not for common view
6. shred	f) personal information

Dealing with phone requests for information

Friends and relatives of patients may phone asking for information about the patient's condition. It is important that patient confidentiality is respected and no information is passed on when it should not be.

Expressions which may be used are:

Can I ask whether you are Mrs Smith's next-of-kin?

Could I ask what relation you are to Mrs Smith?

I'm sorry but I can't pass on any information about Mrs Smith.

I'm afraid I can't discuss Mrs Smith's condition with you but I can tell her you called.

Ex 27: Unscramble the following dialogue between a caller and a staff member. The first line is done for you.

Caller: 'Hello, can you tell me how Mrs Smith's operation went?'

Caller: 'But I'm sure she wouldn't mind, We've been friends for a long time. I have the key to her front door.'

Staff: ' I know it might be difficult for you but I have to respect Mrs Smith's privacy'. I can tell her you called. She may be able to phone you herself.'

Staff: 'I'm sorry but I can't discuss Mrs Smith's case with you.

Caller: 'Oh , I'm her best friend. She'll tell you. I've lived   next door for ten years.'

Caller: ' OK, I understand. Well, can you please tell her Mavis rang and wished her all the best.'

Staff: 'Can I ask whether you are Mrs Smith's relation or next-of-kin?'

Session 4: Developing Activities for Role Play

Many workplace communications lend themselves to role play, for example

- Handovers (stressful, frequent during each shift)

- Passing on patient information e.g after medical review, return from a test

- Talking on the phone – taking messages, phoning other departments

- Procedures e.g checking drugs

Role play is perfect for all situations

- Helps reduce stress – especially for handovers

- Helps improve pronunciation

- Practice of non-verbal communication and cultural sensitivity

- Set up a dialogue template

- Video (with consenting students) – assess communication barriers, personal space

- Can be practised at home

Activity 6: In pairs, think about some of the reasons students may not want to participate in role plays. Then, think of some replies you might give to encourage students to participate.

Some suggestions :

1. It's not serious enough for a classroom activity	
2. We're not studying drama!	
3. We should be concentrating on grammar exercises	
4. It's embarrassing performing in a role play	
5. I'm too shy to do role plays	
6. I don't want to be videoed while I'm doing role plays	

Online resources to help you understand handovers

1. Flinders University Nursing School (Adelaide, Australia)

http://nursing.flinders.edu.au/students/studyaids/clinicalcommunication/page.php?id=11

Click on the handovers and read the transcripts. By moving the mouse over the highlighted

terms you'll hear the pronunciation (Australian accent). These are good examples of

handovers between shifts.

2. NURSING HANDOVER FOR ADULT PATIENTS GUIDELINES
There are four main styles of handover reported in the literature

• Verbal handover

• Tape recorded handover

• Bedside handover

• Written handover

A pre-prepared sheet containing patient details can be used as a method of handover

(Miller, 1998) although this takes time to prepare. A purely verbal handover without

note taking may sometimes be used particularly when time is a factor (Miller, 1998).

However, McKenna (1997) in Sexton et al. (2004) could not identify one single

method as being superior. Situations may vary from one area to another in relation to

numbers of patients, dependency, staffing levels and these factors will also influence

methods selected. A 'mix and match' approach of methods very often may be adopted.

A **safety briefing** (please see appendix 1) is undertaken at the beginning of a shift handover. This should not extend the time of handover, should last only 2-3 minutes and the focus should be the specific patient safety issues for that clinical area on that shift. This information should be carried forward to the next shift and should simply highlight safety as a main priority.

• The Situation, Background, Assessment and Recommendation **(SBAR)** model can be used by any health professional to communicate clinical information about a patient's condition (please see appendix 2).

• Commonly verbal handover is the selected method of handover, be it at the bedside, nurses station or ward office. In order to set a quality standard for each verbal handover, Currie (2002) proposes that each handover should be

'CUBAN':

C onfidential -Ensure information cannot be overheard; notes remain with you all the time and are 'shredded' at the end of the shift. They must not be taken out of the clinical area and must not become part of the patient's case notes.

U ninterrupted -Utilise a quiet area where there are no distractions. Commence on time, at the beginning of the shift.

B rief -Keep information relevant; too much can be confusing. Do not pass on unnecessary or unethical information. Avoid labelling or stereotypes.

A ccurate -Ensure that all information is correct and that no patients are missed out. Care plans should be up to date at the beginning and the end of each shift. Information should be clear and concise and jargon should not be used. Remember bank staff or student nurses may be present.

N amed Nurse -Continuity is essential therefore the person who has looked after the patient should give the handover. Where 12-hour shifts take place, staff may not be on duty for more than two days at a time therefore continuity and more information may be needed.

• Use a structured approach to enable all staff to focus on handing over what is relevant, avoiding overload and passing on irrelevant information. Information relayed should follow the 5 P's rule:

P1 Patient's name, diagnosis, doctor and past relevant history (if this information is not on handover information sheet)

P2 Patient's date/reason for admission and/or date post op

P3 Present restrictions: nil orally (Nil By Mouth) , fluids only, diabetic diet, non-weight bearing etc.

P4 Plan of Care;

The patients main problem/need is………. and will need ……..

The next problem/need is………and will need ………etc

• P5 What part can you play in the next shift? The handover should show

progression (Please see appendix 3 for aide memoir)

Safety Briefing

Health & Safety is EVERYONE'S responsibility, by recording and communicating safety issues we will greatly improve safety for our patients, our colleagues and ourselves.

Safety briefings will highlight areas of concern during the previous shift by informing the on-coming staff of any safety issues and the necessary action taken or required.

The following is a list of examples of issues that should be considered at shift / report handovers to promote and improve patient safety. It is to assist in identifying actual or potential safety risks to patients and does not deter from each individual's responsibility and accountability to safe guard patients whilst in their care. This is not a definitive check list and must not be used as such.

- Risks to patients: e.g. 2 patients with same names
- Near misses
- Incidents
- Post incident learning - reviews / reflection
- Staffing (nursing & medical)
- Patients with mental health issues
- Unauthorised persons / visitors
- Security
- Equipment, faults, etc.
- Unfinished duties at shift change
- Infection control / isolation
- Changes in treatment e.g. drug discontinuation
- Changes in practice e.g. change in lancets for blood glucose testing.
- Estates Referrals e.g. regarding maintenance requests

This is a live record and needs to be accessible to ALL staff on all shifts. The safety briefing record must be retained as evidence that Health & Safety issues have been discussed and communicated at each hand-over where applicable. Incomplete actions must be followed through and may be brought forward on the next briefing sheet.

SBAR REPORTING

State your name and area of work

"I am calling about ……." (Give patient name and location) What it is

"The situation is ………" (Briefly outline the problem) When it started

How severe

MEWS score

SITUATION

"The background is …………."

State admission diagnosis and date of admission

Give brief, relevant medical history and treatment to date

BACKGROUND

"My assessment is ………………"

List changes in the patient's condition, which give cause for concern:

AIRWAY e.g. Is the airway patent? Noisy breathing? Is the patient receiving OXYGEN?

BREATHING e.g. Respiratory rate, breathing pattern, SpO2, skin colour,

CIRCULATION e.g. Pulse rate, rhythm changes, blood pressure, CRT

DISABILITY e.g. AVPU assessment, change in GCS, pain assessment, blood glucose

EXPOSURE e.g. wound drainage, urine output

State here if you are concerned that the patient is rapidly deteriorating and at risk of cardiac arrest

ASSESSMENT

"I recommend that you …… / I would like you to ………."

State what you would like to see done e.g. Come to assess the patient immediately,

Review DNR status; consider transferring the patient to Critical Care

"How long will you be?" (Ensure you are given a time for the patient to be assessed)

"Is there anything specific you would like me to do now?" E.g. CXR, ABG, ECG, Contact Outreach Team

Guidelines for Using the Handover Report Template

Item	Report Inclusion Criteria
1 Patient Name	Always
2 Admission	Date—Recommended
	Complaint—Recommended.
	What brought the patient to the hospital? Nurses will continue to monitor these signs and symptoms.
	Diagnosis--Always
3 Primary MD	Always
4 Significant History	State most significant co-morbidities (e.g., diabetes or CVA). Many patients will have a history too long for shift report. Each institution or unit will need to devise a way to make this information readily accessible to nurses.Ideally, these would be entered into an electronic database and be automatically printed onto the nursing notes/plan of care.
5 Physical Assessment	Resist the temptation to highlight your assessment skills, and state only the abnormal findings which relate significant improvement. Examples:
	* Chest pain patient: State "pain free."
	* Respiratory patient: State "lungs are clear" or describe sounds.
6 Fall Status	State only if patient is at higher risk for falls.
7 Code Status	State any advanced directives or specifications.
8 Capillary Blood Glucose	State those from your shift and interventions.
9 IV	Give the ordered fluid and rate. Optional: Describe infusion site and gauge.

10	I & O	Give only when ordered or significant as a nursing measure.
11	Labs	State only abnormal values. State normal values only when specifically applicable to diagnosis (e.g., normal K after IV runs treatment, normal H&H with a patient who has been bleeding, negative troponi [normal] in a chest pain patient).
12	Timed Events	PRN medications given , Treatments, Events
13	Patient Specific Needs	Any issues not covered with assessment
14	Changes in Condition	Any new clinical findings, improvements or degrading condition
15	Consult	New and/or relevant
16	Current Treatment Plan	Vital--Keep it simple. Example: IV fluids and observe/elevate right leg
17	New Orders	As appropriate, especially related to new treatments or medications the oncoming nurse will need to know
18	Discharge Plans	State "none yet" or give specifics.

Example of a handover sheet

Rm	Name Age Unit Doctor	Dx	Past Hx	MEDICAL Issues & Care	Cognition & Emotional Health	Mobility	ADLs Self Care	Continence	Nutrition & Hydration	Skin Integrity	Expected D/C Date & Plan
Guide				Medical Power of Attorney, NFR Physical observations, Treatment & care	Dementia, ABI, ID, Mental illness, Depression, Delirium, Social isolation, support services, Lives alone, Carer stress Guardian, EPOA, Administrator	Ambulation – aids, Gait & balance probs, Transfers, Falls Mx strategies	Independent, supervision, assistance, aids, dependent- full care	Incontinent – aids, stress / urge probs – requires toileting regime Diarrhoea, constipation Monitoring & Management	Special requirements- thickened fluids, soft food, swallowing / choking probs, dietary / nutritional supplements	Wounds, skin tears, pressure ulcers & care	Return home +/- increased services, to stay with family/ other, Respite, SRS Residential LLC, HLC
1											

Excerpt from 'Cambridge English for Nursing' Intermediate Plus- unit 1

with the permission of the authors Virginia Allum and Patricia McGarr

Charting and documentation: a nursing handover

Healthcare professionals write entries about patients in their care in the Patient Record. The Patient Record documents patient care and, as such, form a permanent legal record of treatment. At the end of each nursing shift, the outgoing nurses give a verbal handover to nurses on the incoming shift. The nurses on the incoming shift are briefed on changes in patient progress and patient care. The handover is usually performed face-to-face but some institutions use recorded handovers. The information which is reported during the handover is gathered from the Patient Record, the Care Plan and any other charts which document specific patient care.

5 a In pairs, discuss the following questions.

1 What do you think are the features of a good handover?
2 What information does not have to be repeated in a handover? Why not?
3 What can happen if handovers do not communicate important information from one shift to another?

b ▶ 1.4 Listen to Emily, the Ward Nurse, handing over a patient, Mrs Cho, and answer the following questions.

1 What is her present medical problem?
2 What is her past medical history?

c ▶ 1.4 Listen again and mark the following statements True (T) or False (F).

1 She does not manage her ADLs at home by herself.
2 She has been quite distressed.
3 Her BP at 10 am was 200/105.
4 Her pulse was 88 at 10 am.
5 The porter has been booked for tomorrow.

d *Abbreviations are often used in both Patient Records and verbal handovers. Some are only found in written documents. It is important to check which abbreviations are approved at the hospital where you are working, as there may be some variance.*

Match the abbreviations (1–14) to their meanings (a–n).

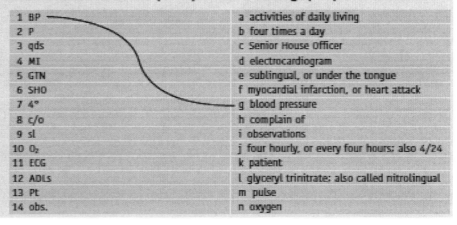

1 BP	a activities of daily living
2 P	b four times a day
3 qds	c Senior House Officer
4 MI	d electrocardiogram
5 GTN	e sublingual, or under the tongue
6 SHO	f myocardial infarction, or heart attack
7 4°	g blood pressure
8 c/o	h complain of
9 sl	i observations
10 O$_2$	j four hourly, or every four hours; also 4/24
11 ECG	k patient
12 ADLs	l glyceryl trinitrate; also called nitrolingual
13 Pt	m pulse
14 obs.	n oxygen

Mrs Cho dialogue

Right, now Mrs Cho in bed number 5. Mrs Cho was readmitted yesterday because of uncontrolled hypertension. You'll probably remember her from last week. She went home last week but couldn't manage her **(1) ADLs** at home by herself. Her daughter had to come in every morning to give her a shower and help her during the day. She has been quite distressed about it according to her daughter. She presented to the unit with uncontrolled hypertension despite a change in medication. She has a past history of **(2) MI** this year in June. Ah... This morning she complained of chest pain. The **(3) RMO** was called. Her **(4)BP** at the time, um.. that was...10am this morning ...was 210 over 105 and her pulse was 100. She had an **(5)ECG** done and was given **(6) GTN** sublingually. We gave her some **(7) O$_2$** via the mask and she seemed to settle. She's for cardiac catheterisation tomorrow to assess the extent of the damage to her heart. I've booked the porter already. Strict **(8)4/24** BP and Pulse and report any chest pain immediately of course. She's had no chest pain this shift.

A note on *'complained of'*

Some terms which used to be commonly used are being reviewed in the light of the negative connotations they are thought to portray. Terms such as:

- *complain of*

- *presenting complaint*

- *sufferer e.g AIDS sufferer*

- *victim e.g stroke victim*

'complain of' is replaced with an objective statement e.g 'Patient reported a pain level of 5

'presenting complaint' is replaced with 'presenting symptom'

'sufferer' replaced with 'patient has AIDS'

'suffers from' is acceptable when talking about chronic conditions e.g 'Patient suffers from chronic pain'

Phone calls

- Asking for info e.g lab results
- Making a referral e.g. to a peripheral hospital
- Making an appointment
- Taking calls from friends and relations – (Data Protection issues)
- Calling for medical assistance – using SBAR

Cambridge English for Nursing Intermediate +

with permission from the authors Virginia Allum and Patricia McGarr

Telephone skills: contacting other staff

4 a In pairs, discuss the following questions.
1 What hospital communication systems are you familiar with?
2 What do you think are the features of a good communication system?
3 How is technology changing the way we communicate in the workplace?

b ▶ 5.3 Listen to a telephone conversation between Frances and Dr Sinclair, an SHO, and mark the following statements True (T) or False (F).
1 Frances calls Dr Sinclair to check on the results of Mrs Faisal's urine test.
2 Dr Sinclair asks Frances to remind her about Mrs Faisal's diagnosis.
3 The doctor has decided not to prescribe antibiotics.
4 A midstream urine specimen has been collected from the patient but the nurse needs the doctor to sign a Pathology Form.

c ▶ 5.3 Listen to the conversation again and complete the following extract.

Frances:	It's Frances from eight west here. I'm (1) _Calling_ _about_ one of your patients, Mrs Faisal.
Dr Sinclair:	Er, Mrs Faisal? Can you (2) _____ _____ ?
Frances:	Yeah, she was admitted two days ago, er ...
Dr Sinclair:	Yeah, I remember. Isn't she (3) _____ _____ the removal of an ovarian cyst?
Frances:	Yeah, that's the patient. I think she may have a UTI. She's (4) _____ _____ frequency, urgency and pain when she passes urine.
Dr Sinclair:	Right. Is she (5) _____ ?
Frances:	Yeah, her temp's (6) _____ _____ _____ . She's around thirty-seven point eight. She doesn't feel brilliant either – general (7) _____ .
Dr Sinclair:	... Can you take an (8) _____ and I'll come over and (9) _____ some antibiotics.
Frances:	The MSU's already done, but I'll leave the (10) _____ _____ at the desk to be signed. Then we can send it to Pathology...

d In pairs, practise the telephone conversation. Student A, you are Frances; Student B, you are Dr Sinclair. Remember to use the strategies for clarification and checking understanding. Swap roles and practise again.

Transcript of 5.3

Frances: Hello, is that Dr Sinclair?

Dr Sinclair: Yes, it is

Frances: Oh hello, it's Frances from 8 West here. I'm calling about one of your patients, Mrs
Faisal.

Dr Sinclair: Er, Mrs Faisal? Can you remind me?

Frances: Yeah, she was admitted two days ago, er …

Dr Sinclair: Yeah, I remember. Isn't she in for the removal of an ovarian cyst?

Frances: Yeah, that's the patient. I think she may have a UTI. She's complaining of frequency,
urgency and pain when she passes urine.

Dr Sinclair: Right. Is she febrile?

Frances: Yeah, her temp's up a bit. She's around thirty-seven point eight. She doesn't feel brilliant
either – general malaise.

Dr Sinclair: OK. She's got frequency, urgency, pain and she's febrile. Can you take an MSU and
I'll come over and write up some antibiotics.

Frances: The MSU's already done, but I'll leave the Pathology Form at the desk to be signed. Then
we can send it to Pathology. I've encouraged her to increase her fluid intake too.

Dr Sinclair: Great, thanks. I'm just on 8 East at the moment. I'll probably be up there in fifteen
minutes.

Frances: Thanks. See you.

This article is about giving information over the phone (telenursing)

http://www.medscape.com/viewarticle/415062_3

Potential Telecommunication Risks: Cautions and Suggestions for the Team

from Progress in Cardiovascular Nursing

Communication Risks For Nurses

Traditionally, nurses have been educated to care for patients in a hospital setting, with public health or home health nursing addressed in a semester course. Our assessment skills have been focused on direct care, with visual prompts to guide our practice. Accepting a phone call from a patient or family member renders the nurse legally accountable for the advice given.[7] Standard protocols and documentation are important aspects of telenursing. Leaving a message for a patient on a voicemail service or on a machine is not acceptable. It is the nurse's responsibility to speak directly to a patient when delivering instructions or responding to a patient's phone message. Telephone conversations, voice messages, e-mail communication, and faxes do not allow us the opportunity to use visual cues in our assessments. Therefore, it is important to speak to the patient so one can probe areas of concern. Several risks may be encountered with telenursing. These risks include misunderstandings, absence of standard protocols for telephone triage, incomplete documentation, and multi-state practice issues.

Tips for Getting People to Slow Down!

from http://esl.about.com/od/businessspeakingskills/a/t_tips.htm

One of the biggest problems is speed. Native speakers, especially business people, tend to speak very quickly on the telephone. Here are some practical tips to get native speakers of English to slow down! Immediately ask the person to speak slowly.

► When taking note of a name or important information, repeat each piece of information as the person speaks. This is an especially effective tool. By repeating each important piece of information or each number or letter as the spell or give you a telephone number you automatically slow the speaker down.

► Do not say you have understood if you have not. Ask the person to repeat until you have understood. Remember that the other person needs to make himself/herself understood and it is in his/her interest to make sure that you have understood. If you ask a person to explain more than twice they will usually slow down.

Key phrases

► Good morning, this is Britta Grey calling from Germany.

► I'd like to speak to Mr/Ms Jones, please.

► I'd like to leave a message for ...

► Just a moment, please. I'll put you through.

► I'm sorry, the line's busy / engaged.

► Would you like to call back later?

► I'm afraid she's not in the office today.

► I'm afraid he's away on business.

► Can I take a message?

► Can she call you back when she gets in?

► I'm calling about …

► I'm returning your call.

► I'll get back to you on that.

► I'll give her the message as soon as possible.

► Can we fix an appointment?

► Does Thursday suit you?

► Let me check my diary.

► Sorry, I didn't catch that.

► What was your name again, please?

► Could you speak more slowly, please?

► Could you spell that for me, please?

► Thanks for your help.

► I look forward to hearing from you soon.

► Thank you. Bye.

► You're welcome. Bye.

► Am I disturbing you?

► I am on another line?

► Could I take your name please

► Hang on, I'll put you through (very informal)

Activity : In pairs, think about other phrases which may be used on the phone in a healthcare environment

A very interesting article about the problems relatives and friends of patients have when calling the ward for information.

Excerpt:

A short questionnaire was designed following numerous discussions with members of the public who had telephoned a nursing department either on their own behalf or for others.

In this instance, a nursing department was defined as a hospital ward or a community nursing unit, which might include, for example, a school nursing setting or a hospice.

Respondents were asked to analyse their experiences of instances when they telephoned to speak to a nurse. These items were frequently cited as being of most concern for callers:

•   Feeling you weren't being a nuisance

•   Being informed of the name of the department/unit which answers your call

•   Knowing the name and job title of the person you were speaking to

•   Having your queries dealt with efficiently

•   Having your call answered quickly

•   Not being cut off

•   Having your call redirected to the correct department.

Leaving a Message

Sometimes, there may not be anyone to answer the telephone and you will need to leave a message. Follow this outline to make sure that the person who should receive your message has all the information he/she needs.

1. Introduction - - - - Hello, this is Ken. OR Hello, My name is Ken Beare (more formal).

2. State the time of day and your reason for calling - - - - - It's ten in the morning. I'm phoning (calling, ringing) to find out if ... / to see if ... / to let you know that ... / to tell you that ...

3. Make a request - - - - Could you call (ring, telephone) me back? / Would you mind ... ? /

4. Leave your telephone number - - - - My number is .... / You can reach me at .... / Call me at ...

5. Finish - - - - Thanks a lot, bye. / I'll talk to you later, bye.

Here's an example of message

Telephone: (Ring... Ring... Ring...) Hello, this is Tom. I'm afraid I'm not in at the moment. Please leave a message after the beep..... (beep)

Ken: Hello Tom, this is Ken. It's about noon and I'm calling to see if you would like to go to the Mets game on Friday. Could you call me back? You can reach me at 367-8925 until five this afternoon. I'll talk to you later, bye.

As you can see, leaving a message is pretty simple. You only need to make sure that you have stated all the most important information: Your Name, The Time, The Reason for Calling, Your Telephone Number

Day 3

1: Developing Activities for Effective Listening Skills

2: Authentic Materials II: Use of Video in EMP

3: Effective Patient Communication Skills I: Gathering Information

4: Effective Communication Skills II: Examining the Patient

Day 3

1: Developing Activities for Effective Listening Skills

Use :

• health websites

• nursing and medical student websites

• pharma websites

Keep in mind the process of material writing

from 'Materials Development in Language Teaching' edited by Brian Tomlinson p 112

Figure 5.1

IDENTIFICATION by teacher or learner(s) of a need to fulfil or a problem to solve by

the creation of materials

EXPLORATION of the area of need / problem in terms of what language, what

meanings, what functions, what skills, etc

CONTEXTUAL REALISATION of the proposed new materials by the finding of

suitable ideas, contexts or texts with which to work

PEDAGOGICAL REALISATION of materials by the findings of appropriate exercises

and activities AND the writing of appropriate instructions for use

PHYSICAL PRODUCTION of materials, involving consideration of layout, type size,

visuals, reproduction, tape length etc

Reusable Learning Objects (RLOs) available for use – The Nottingham Nursing School resources

http://www.nottingham.ac.uk/nmp/sonet/rlos/rlolist.php

Alcohol as a public health issue	This learning resource will increase your knowledge and understanding of how alcohol impacts on public health in a physical, psychological and social way.	Healthcare (general), Healthy Living	ⓘ
Alcohol Identification and Brief Advice	This learning resource introduces the concept of IBA (Identification and Brief Advice) and demonstrates the importance of communication skills and an informal approach when using AUDIT and delivering brief advice.	Healthcare (general), Healthy Living	ⓘ
An introduction to receptor pharmacology	To describe the different types of receptor which drugs target.	Pharmacology	ⓘ
Aseptic Non-Touch Technique	Introduces the concept of ANTT, used to prevent infection during clinical procedures; includes a video demonstration.	Practice learning and clinical skills	ⓘ
Asking the right question	This RLO outlines why asking the right question can help in the search for evidence, and explains how to construct good questions using the PICO technique.	EBP, Research methods	ⓘ

Nottingham Nursing School Video example

Resource: The resource section provides:

• a glossary of terms

• a click and drag activity

• a video demonstration

ANTT Basics

Aseptic Non-Touch Technique (ANTT) aims to prevent **micro-organisms** on hands, surfaces or equipment from being introduced to a **susceptible** site such as a **surgical wound**, **catheter** or **central venous line**.

The ANTT has a long history in health care practice, and is most commonly associated with **wound care**. However, the nature and scope of ANTT is dependant (sic) on the procedure that is to be performed. For example, when accessing **peripheral cannulae**, the principles of ANTT should be followed, but **dressing packs** and sterile gloves may not be necessary. However, the overriding and basic principle is that the susceptible site should not come into contact with any item that is not **sterile**.

Hint: check the transcript for spelling errors before printing out for students. For example, *dependent* was incorrectly spelled 'dependant' (see above).

Before you and your students start, check you understand the **bold** terms

micro-organisms
susceptible
surgical wound
catheter
central venous line.
wound care
peripheral cannulae
dressing packs
sterile

Activity 7: Students do the click and drag activity at home to prepare.

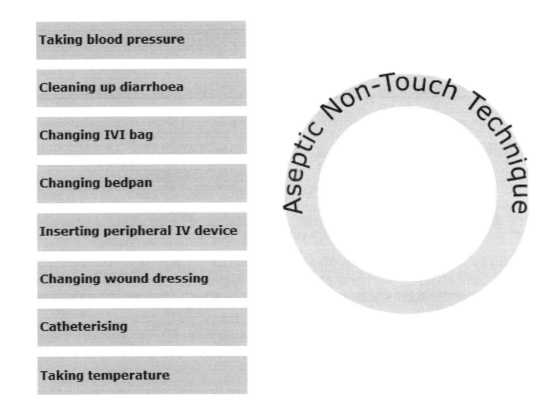

In class, students explain which activities use Aseptic Non-Touch Technique. (ANTT – say 'Ant') . Students ask whether ANTT is necessary for the listed activities. For example,

Student A: Do you have to use ANTT when you take a blood pressure reading?

Student B: No, when you take a blood pressure reading, you don't have to use ANTT.

Student A: Do you have to use ANTT when you change an IVI bag ?

Student B: Yes, when you change an IVI bag, you have to use ANTT.

Using resources from Talking Medicine website

Is perinatal HIV infection reversible?

http://www.english-talking-medicine.com/HIV-infection.html

Source: Talking Medicine, 1995

Listen two or three times before reading the transcript. The more you listen, the more you will understand.

The case of an infant who was found to be HIV-positive **shortly** after birth and who subsequently cleared the virus, raised some **intriguing** questions about perinatally-acquired HIV infection. The child was born in Los Angeles to a woman who had been diagnosed as having asymptomatic HIV-1 infection during the fourth month of pregnancy. At birth, the child tested negative but at 19 and again at 51 days, HIV-1 was detected in his peripheral blood mononuclear cells. However, at 12 months of age, the child was again seronegative, and numerous subsequent tests over the past five years have also been negative, providing evidence of clearance of the virus.

An estimated 30 to 40 percent of HIV-infected mothers transmit the virus to their infants, and the majority of the infants will then **go on** to develop symptoms of AIDS within a few years. Several hypotheses have been put forward to explain this observation, the most **plausible** of which are the presence of a defective virus or the elimination of the virus by the child's immune system. At any rate, understanding the mechanism of clearance, whether it is based on the biologic nature of the virus or the immune response of the host, could have **profound** implications for HIV-1 therapy and vaccine design.

See blue highlighted Words and Expressions: (I've made them **bold**)

short•ly

If you say that something happened shortly after another event, you mean that it happened

soon after.

"The patient was released from hospital shortly after the operation".

in•tri•guing

If you describe something as intriguing, you mean that it is interesting or strange.

"This intriguing book is both thoughtful and informative".

go on to

If you go on to do something, you do it after you have done another thing.

"Most patients who are infected with HIV go on to develop AIDS".

plau•sible

an explanation or statement that is plausible seems likely to be true or valid.

"With cough and fever, the diagnosis of a respiratory tract infection was plausible".

pro•found

you use profound to emphasize the great degree or intensity of something.

"Antibiotics have had a profound effect on the mortality rates for infectious diseases".

Activity 8: Developing extension activities from the listening exercise:

In pairs, students read the transcript and find all the medical terms which include the prefixes

or word parts:

peri- (around)_____

peri- (around) _____

natal (birth) _____

a- (without) _____

mono- (one) _____

sero- (blood) _____

hypo- (under) _____

bio- (life) _____

-ology (study of) _____

Through exposure to authentic scenarios of patient interactions, learners experience examples of authentic language in an authentic setting. This session will look at how video can be used to meet the real needs of medical professionals; illustrating how the medium enables trainers to highlight and develop understanding of all the elements of communication as well as their implications for effective patient interactions in English. As well as looking at hospital and medical equipment company training videos, we will also consider the use of TV medical dramas in the EMP classroom.

Useful Links:

Geeky Medics   www.geekymedics.com/2010/09/29/cardiovascular-examination-2/

This is a fabulous resource made by a self confessed 'Geeky Medic' ! The video is an example of how a medical student would undertake an OSCE -this video is for the respiratory system but there are others.

OSCE: Respiratory Examination

http://geekymedics.com/osce/respiratory-examination-2/

The video includes a complete transcript of the video.

Introduction

Introduce yourself

Explain what you would like to examine

Gain Consent

Expose chest

Position at 45°

Ask patient if they have pain anywhere before you begin!

General Inspection

General appearance

Any treatments or adjuncts around bed - o2, inhalers, nebulisers, sputum pots

Does patient look SOB? - nasal flaring, pursed lips, accessory muscles

Scars

Cyanosis

Chest Wall - abnormalities or asymmetry - barrel chest (COPD)

Cachexia

Cough or Wheeze – ask to cough & assess nature (productive or dry)

Hands

Check temperature

Clubbing

Nicotine Staining

Wasting of the dorsal interossi (pancoast tumour)

Fine tremor – b2 agonist use

Flapping tremor - CO2 retention

Pulse – rate & rhythm

Pulse Paradoxus - pulse volume decreases with inspiration

Respiratory rate

Head & Neck

Conjunctival pallor - anaemia

Horner's syndrome - ptosis, small pupil, enopthalmos (sunken eye) & loss of sweating

Central cyanosis

JVP - elevated in cor-pulmonale & severe bronchitis

Close inspection of thorax

Scars - lateral (thoracotomy)

Asymmetry - seen in lung removal

Deformities - barrel chest, pectus excavatum & carniatum

Palpation

Crico-sternal distance

Tracheal position

Apex beat

Chest Expansion

Percussion

Compare side to side

Supraclavicular

Infraclavicular

Chest

Axilla

Auscultate

Compare side to side

Assess volume & quality - vesicular or bronchial

Vocal resonance

Repeat Inspection, Chest Expansion, Percussion & Auscultation

To complete my examination

Thank patient

Wash hands

Summarise Findings

Say you would; Do a full cardiovascular examination if indicated

Activity 9: In pairs, discuss:

1. What you might need to review before watching the OSCE?

2. How would you use the OSCE in a class?

3. How would you use the OSCE video to 'win over' any of your students who may feel ambivalent about role play

Nursing 411   www.nursing411.org/Free_Videos.html

A small selection of videos showing nursing procedures.

This session will focus on taking a patient history for the patient interview or nursing assessment which includes creating rapport, setting the agenda and making use of effective question techniques and dealing with sensitive issues.

Excerpt from English for Medical Purposes: Doctors

Unit 3 : Starting the patient interview

    Aims:

- Starting the patient interview

- Asking questions used during a patient interview

- Using different questions to understand the patient's problem

- Prepositions used with the past simple

- Using the past simple and past continuous to ask about symptoms

- Asking about symptoms

- Using medical terminology versus everyday terms

Starting the patient interview

Ex 1: Before you start, answer the following questions:

1. Where can you get information about the patient's complaint?

2. Why are closed questions useful when interviewing patients? e.g *When did the pain start?*

3. Is it a good thing for patients to research their illness on the internet?

Read the text below. Then, answer the questions which follow.

Types of questions which are used during a patient interview:

During a patient interview, open questions, closed questions, questions with options and summarising questions are used to help get as much information as possible from patients.

Open questions

Open questions 'open up' the conversation. They allow the speaker to start giving information about what it troubling them. The patient interview should start with an open question. For example, *Can you tell me a bit about the pain you've been having?*

Closed questions

Closed questions are questions which used ask for specific information from a patient. They usually get a reply like '*Yes*' or *'No'*. For example, *Do you have any allergies?* Answer: *Yes*

Questions with options

Questions with options give one or two possible answers. The questions may clarify a previous answer if it is not clear what the patient meant. For example,

Patient: *I've got yellow fluid coming out of my wound.*

Doctor: *Do you mean fluid which is almost clear and doesn't smell or a thick, yellow discharge which smells bad?*

The doctor asks the question which offers two possibilities to check whether the patient is referring to normal haemoserous fluid or pus indicating an infection.

Summarising questions

After listening to the patient, summarising questions can be used to ensure that the doctor feels confident that s/he has understood the patient correctly. For example,

Doctor: *So, from what I understand, you've been losing weight and feeling sick for several weeks now. Is that about right?'*

Ex 2: Complete the following statements. Use the words in the box below

summarising questions   open questions   question with options

Closed questions

1. Doctors should start patient interviews with _____ so patients feel they can talk about their problems.

2. _____ are used to get facts or quick answers from patients.

3. It is a good idea to use _____ to repeat what a patient says so it is clear what the patient is saying.

4. Asking a patient a _____ is often useful if the patient is embarrassed about talking about a problem.

Ex 3: In pairs, put the following questions under the correct headings.

Where did you cut yourself?   How can I help you today?

Did you lose consciousness?   Can you tell me a bit about your problem

Does the wound smell?   How did you fall?   When did you fall?

What does the cut look like?   What seems to be the problem?

Open questions	Closed questions

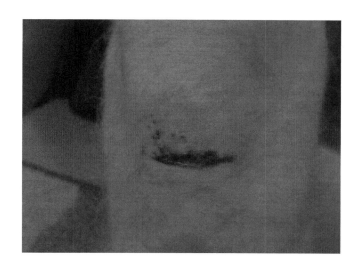

Using different types of questions to understand the patient's problem

Read the dialogue between a doctor and a patient. Answer the questions which follow.

Doctor: Hello, Mrs Smith. What seems to be the problem?

       Patient: Well, I wasn't paying attention and I fell over and cut myself.

Doctor: I see. How did you fall?

Patient: It was silly really. I tripped over my suitcase.

Doctor: When did you fall?

Patient: Two days ago.

Doctor: What does the wound look like?

Patient: I'm a bit worried because it looks yellow.

Doctor: Does it smell?

Patient: Yes, it does.

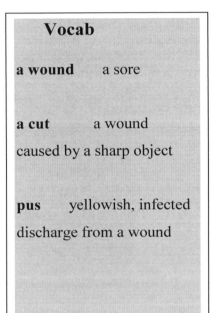

Vocab	
a wound	a sore
a cut	a wound caused by a sharp object
pus	yellowish, infected discharge from a wound

Ex 4:
1. What happened to Mrs Smith?

2. How did she injure herself?

3. When did she injure herself?

4. Why is Mrs Smith concerned about the wound?

Prepositions used with the past simple

Review the prepositions (or absence of preposition) used with time expressions

at	at 4 o'clock	at the end of the week
around	around 3.30	
on	on Monday	on March 19th
in	in January	in 2009
(no prep)	a few days + ago	yesterday

Ex 5: Complete the following dialogue excerpts.

Before you start, review the following terms relating to symptoms

pain	unpleasant feeling
indigestion	heartburn
vomiting	bringing up food
diarrhoea	passing loose stool

5am	three days	Monday	yesterday

Doctor: When did the pain start in your shoulder?

Patient: It started (1) _____ ago when I was lifting a heavy suitcase.

Doctor: When did the indigestion get worse?

Patient: It got worse (2) _____.

Doctor: When did you start vomiting?

Patient: At (3) _____.

Doctor: When did you first notice the diarrhoea?

Patient: It was on (4) _____.

Using the past simple and past continuous to talk about symptoms

Past simple v past continuous

The past simple is often used to describe a past action which is finished or completed.

I hurt myself yesterday

I cut myself this morning

I fell over a week ago

I hurt my shoulder last month

The past continuous is used to describe a background action which was going on at the time of another action

I was walking in the park when I tripped over a rock

I was running along the beach when I fell over

I was getting into the bath when I slipped over

I was going into the shop when I crashed into some shelving

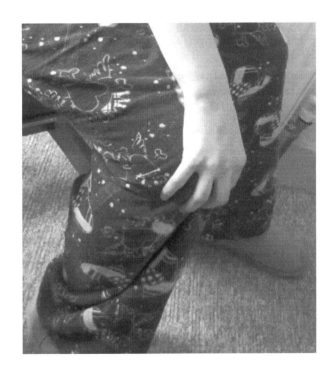

Ex 6: In pairs, role play the following dialogues. There are two scenarios to practise. Student A: you are the doctor. Ask Student B (patient) a question. Student B, select the correct answers. Then, swap roles.

Role Card : **Doctor**

Doctor: What can I help you with?

Patient: _____

Doctor: OK. What were you doing when you hurt it?

Patient: _____

Doctor: When did you hurt it?

Patient: _____

Role Card : **Patient**

I hurt my elbow

 I was out walking when I tripped on the pavement.

 I hurt it this morning.

I was having a shower when I slipped over.

I hurt my knee.

I hurt it yesterday evening.

Patient-centred interviews versus Doctor-centred interviews

In patient-centred interviews, patients explain why they have visited the doctor. They are able to talk uninterrupted and explain their symptoms as they experience them. In doctor-centred interviews doctors may diagnose their patient's condition after reading the patient notes and only listening briefly to what patients have to say.

Asking about symptoms

The present perfect continuous is used to describe past actions which may be seen as taking a long time to complete. Examples are

I've *been feeling* sick for a few days

I've *been vomiting* for a day

I've *been coughing* for a few days

My eye's *been itching* for a few days

I've *been suffering* from constipation for a week

Replies to questions starting *How long have you been..?*

have been + past participle → **for** (used for a period of time)	
have been + past participle → **since** (used for when the period of time started)	
for 10 minutes	**since** 2006
for 2 months	**since** Friday
for a long time	**since** last week

Ex 7: Match the questions 1- 6 with the correct answer a-f

Doctor	Patient
1. How long have you been feeling sick?	a) I've been coughing for several days
2. How long have you been vomiting?	b) I've been suffering from constipation since Thursday
3. How long has your eye been itching?	c) I've been bleeding for two and a half weeks
4. How long have you been coughing?	d) I've been vomiting since yesterday
5. How long have you been suffering from constipation?	e) It's been itching for a few days
6. How long have you been bleeding?	f) I've been feeling sick since I arrived last week

Ex 8: Select the correct verb form to complete the following excerpts of dialogues between a doctor and a patient

Doctor: How long have you been feeling sick?

Patient: I've been feeling sick for a few days.

Doctor: When (1) **did you start** / **have you started** feeling sick

Patient: I (2) **started** / **have started** feeling sick on Friday.

Doctor: How long have your ears been discharging pus?

Patient: They've been discharging pus for around two days.

Doctor: In which ear (3) **was** the discharge **worse** / **has** the discharge **been worse**?

Patient: It (4) **was** / **has been** worse in the left ear.

Doctor: How long have you been coughing?

Patient: I've been coughing since Wednesday.

Doctor: When (5) **did** the cough **become** productive / **has** the cough **become** productive?

Patient: Mm, it (6) **became** productive / **has become** productive yesterday

Ex 9: Role play. Use the role play cards (Doctor and Patient) to role play the following dialogue. Student A, you are the doctor. Student B, you are the patient. Student A, question the patient. Student B , select the correct answer.

Doctor Role Card

Doctor: How long have you been feeling faint?

Patient: _____

Doctor: When did you start feeling faint?

Patient: _____

Doctor: What were you doing when you first started feeling faint?

Patient: _____

Patient Role Card

I've been suffering from high blood pressure for years

I've been feeling faint for a few days.

I was playing golf when I felt unwell.

I started feeling faint on Friday.

I was at the beach all day.

 I started having blood pressure problems in 2009

Ex 10: Student A, write the questions to match the answers which Student B (patient) gives. The answers are in the Patient Role Card above. The first question is done for you.

Doctor: How long have you been suffering from blood pressure problems?

Patient: I've been _____

Doctor: When _____?

Patient: I started _____

Doctor: What _____?

Patient: I was   _____

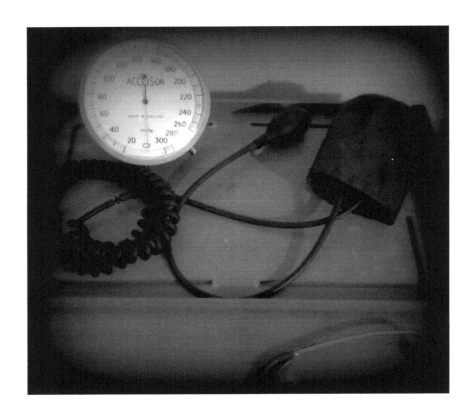

Using medical terminology or everyday language when talking to patients

Ex 11: Before you start, in pairs, answer the following questions

1. Do you try to use everyday terms so patients can understand you?

2. Do you think doctors should use medical terms to reassure their patients about their professionalism?

3. Should patients be allowed to have the right to decide their own treatment or should their doctor make all the decisions?

Read the following text and then answer the questions which follow.

In English, medical terminology is not generally used in everyday language. Most patients will understand everyday terms but may not understand medical terms.

By using medical terms instead of everyday terms when explaining diseases or treatment to patients you may set up a **communication barrier.** A communication barrier is something which stops the easy flow of communication or information-sharing between people.

Communication barriers may also have the effect of stopping patients from really hearing what you are saying. It might increase their anxiety levels if they are concerned that they have not understood key parts of your instructions.

12: Answer the following questions True / False

1. Most patients are familiar with medical terminology   True / False

2. Communication barriers may prevent patients from following a doctor's instructions.

          True / False

3. It is important to make patients feel at ease by speaking to them in a way they can

understand.   True / False

Ex 13: Match the medical terms 1- 8 with their equivalent everyday expression a-h

medical terminology	everyday expression
1. hypertension	a) fever
2. hypotension	b) itchiness
3. tachycardia	c) sick feeling
4. bradycardia	d) low blood pressure
5. pyrexia	e) high blood pressure
6. hyperglycaemia	f) fast pulse
7. nausea	g) slow pulse
8. urticaria	h) high blood sugar

Explaining medical terms to patients

Sometimes you may need to use a medical term and then have to explain the meaning

of the term to a patient. To explain terms, you'll use expressions like:

What this means is that....

(medical term) means...

(medical term) is the same as

Ex 14: Complete the following excerpts using the words from the box below

high blood sugars	fever	high blood
pressure		

Doctor: Have you had hypertension?

Patient: Um, what's that?

Doctor: Have you ever had (1) _____before?

Patient: Oh, no I haven't.

Doctor: Do you suffer from hyperglycaemia?

Patient: What do you mean?

Doctor: Have you ever had (2) _____before?

Patient: Oh, yes I do sometimes.

Doctor: Have you had any pyrexia in the last week?

Patient: I'm sorry, I don't understand what that means?

Doctor: I mean, have you had a (3) _____?

Patient: No, I haven't.

Ex 15: Complete the following excerpts using the terms in the box below

fast pulse	itchiness	nausea

Doctor: Where is the urticaria?

Patient: I'm sorry, I don't understand what you mean.

Doctor: Oh right, I mean where is the (1) _____?

Patient: It's on my back

Doctor: Hello, Mr Brown. Do you have any (2) _____today?

Patient: What do you mean?

Doctor: I was asking if you have any sick feeling today ?

Patient: Yes, I've been feeling unwell all morning.

Doctor: Good Morning. Are you still tachycardic today?

Patient: What do you mean?

Doctor: I'm sorry, I was asking if you still have a (3) _____today?

Patient: No, it seems to be OK today

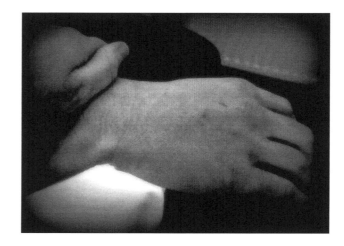

Ex 16: In pairs, place the dialogue in the correct order. Then, role play the dialogue with your partner. Student A, you are the doctor. Student B, you are the patient.

Doctor: Good Morning, Mrs Smith. How are you feeling today?

Patient: Oh, I see. Yes. I had a fever earlier this morning.

Doctor: I'm sorry. What I mean to ask is whether you have had a high temperature this morning.

Doctor: OK. But you don't have a high temperature now?

Patient: Not too bad, thanks, doctor.

Doctor: Have you had any more episodes of pyrexia this morning?

Patient: I'm not sure what you mean.

Patient: No. I seem to be all right now.

Vocab
episode of …   a period of time when a patient suffers from a symptom
suffer from   to experience a symptom or disease

Role Play card: doctor

Doctor: Good Morning,_____. _____?

Patient:

Doctor: Have you _____?

Patient:

Doctor: I'm _____. _____

_____

Patient:

Doctor: OK. _____?

Patient:

Role Play card: patient

Doctor:

Patient: Not _____

Doctor:

Patient: I'm _____?

Doctor:

Patient: Oh, _____ . _____.

Doctor:

Patient: No. _____.

Answers

Ex 1:

1. From the patient, the patient's relatives, the patient record,old medical records,from the patient's GP

2. To get factual information or'quick' information

3. Answers will vary: For: better health literacy, doctor does not have to explain basic information to patient so saves time,patient takes part in own treatment options. Against: patients may not understand information or information may not relate to their condition,websites may not be reliable,websites may be advertising sites pushing a particular treatment or surgery.

Ex 2:

1. Doctors should start patient interviews with open questions so patients feel they can talk about their problems.

2. Closed questions are used to get facts or quick answers from patients.

3. It is a good idea to use summarising questions to repeat what a patient says so it is clear what the patient is saying.

4. Asking a patient questions with options is often useful if the patient is embarrassed about talking about a problem.

Ex 3 Open questions

How can I help you today?

What seems to be the problem?

Can you tell me a bit about your problem?

How did you fall?

What does the cut look like?

Closed questions

Where did you cut yourself?

Did you lose consciousness?

When did you fall?

Does the wound smell?

Ex 4:

1. fell over and cut herself   2. tripped over suitcase

3. 2 days ago   4. looks yellow and smells

Ex 5

Doctor: When did the pain start in your shoulder?

Patient: It started three days ago when I was lifting a heavy suitcase.

Doctor: When did the indigestion get worse?

Patient: It got worse yesterday.

Doctor: When did you start vomiting?

Patient: At 5am.

Doctor: When did you first notice the diarrhoea?

Patient: It was on Monday.

Role Play 1

Doctor: What can I help you with?

Patient: I hurt my elbow

Doctor: OK. What were you doing when you hurt it?

Patient: I was having a shower when I slipped over.

Doctor: When did you hurt it?

Patient: I hurt it yesterday evening.

Role Play 2

Doctor: What can I help you with?

Patient: I hurt my knee.

Doctor: OK. What were you doing when you hurt it?

Patient: I was out walking when I tripped on the pavement.

Doctor: When did you hurt it?

Patient: I hurt it this morning

Ex 7:   1.f   2.d   3.e   4.a   5.b   6.c

Ex 8:

Doctor: How long have you been feeling sick?

Patient: I've been feeling sick for a few days.

Doctor: When (1) **did you start** feeling sick

Patient: I (2)   **started**   feeling sick on Friday.

Doctor: How long have your ears been discharging pus?

Patient: They've been discharging pus for around two days.

Doctor: In which ear (3) **was** the discharge **worse** ?

Patient: It (4) **was** worse in the left ear.

Doctor: How long have you been coughing?

Patient: I've been coughing since Wednesday.

Doctor: When (5) **did** the cough **become** productive ?

Patient: Mm, it (6) **became** productive productive yesterday

Ex 9:

Doctor: How long have you been feeling faint?

Patient: I've been feeling faint for a few days.

Doctor: When did you start feeling faint?

Patient: I started feeling faint on Friday.

Doctor: What were you doing when you first started feeling faint?

Patient: I was at the beach all day.

Ex 10:

Doctor: How long have you been suffering from blood pressure problems?

Patient: I've been suffering from high blood pressure for years

Doctor: When did you start having blood pressure problems?

Patient: I started having blood pressure problems in 2009

Doctor: What were you doing when you had the problems?

Patient: I was playing golf when I felt unwell.

Ex 11: Answers will vary

Ex 12:

1. False 2. True 3. True

Ex 13: 1.e 2.d 3.f 4.g 5.a 6.h 7.c 8.b

Ex 14: 1. high blood pressure 2. high blood sugars 3. fever

Ex 15:

Doctor: Where is the urticaria?

Patient: I'm sorry, I don't understand what you mean.

Doctor: Oh right, I mean where is the itchiness?

Patient: It's on my back

Doctor: Hello, Mr Brown. Do you have any nausea today?

Patient: What do you mean?

Doctor: I was asking if you have any sick feeling today ?

Patient: Yes, I've been feeling unwell all morning.

Doctor: Good Morning. Are you still tachycardic today?

Patient: What do you mean?

Doctor: I'm sorry, I was asking if you still have a fast pulse today?

Patient: No, it seems to be OK today.

Ex 16:

Doctor: Good Morning, Mrs Smith. How are you feeling today?

Patient: Not too bad, thanks, doctor.

Doctor: Have you had any more episodes of pyrexia this morning?

Patient: I'm not sure what you mean.

Doctor: I'm sorry. What I mean to ask is whether you have had a high temperature this morning.

Patient: Oh, I see. Yes. I had a fever earlier this morning.

Doctor: OK. But you don't have a high temperature now?

Patient: No. I seem to be all right now.

Excerpt from 'English for Medical Purposes: Doctors' by Virginia Allum

Unit 6: Examining a patient

- Respecting Privacy and Patient Confidentiality
- Asking a patient to undress or remove a piece of clothing
- Verbs of movement
- Phrasal verbs versus formal terms
- Using commands – breath in and hold your breath/ don't move/ emergency situations/ during tests

Examination of a patient: Language used

- verbs of movement

- language of giving instruction

- polite instructions

- putting patients at ease

- respecting dignity and privacy when examining patients

- cultural sensitivity

Ex 4: Complete the following statements using verbs in the box below

roll up	unbutton	take off	roll up

1. The doctor asks the patient to _____ her shirt so he can listen to her heart.

2. The doctor asks the patient if she could _____ her sleeve so he can take some blood.

3. The doctor instructs the patient to _____ her trousers so he can check her ankles for swelling.

4. The doctor wants the patient to _____ her shoes so he can look at her feet.

Ex 5: Complete the verbs for undressing 1- 7 with the correct parts of clothing a- g

1. unbutton	a) your trousers, your skirt
2. roll up	b) your top, your tee-shirt, your shirt, your skirt
3. lift up	c) your coat, your socks, your shoes, your jacket
4. pull down	d) your shirt
5. take off	e) your sleeve, your jeans, your trousers
6. open	f) your trousers, your underwear, your skirt
7. unzip	g) your jacket

Ex 6: Complete the statements using the opposite verb to the verb used

in the first instruction.

put on	zip up	roll down	put down	button up	do up

1. Could you unbutton your shirt, please? You can _____ it _____ again now.

2. Could you roll up your sleeve, please? You can _____ it _____ again now.

3. Would you lift up your top? You can _____ it _____ now.

4. Would you please take off your jacket? You can _____ it _____ now.

5. Would you open your shirt, please? You can _____ it _____ again.

6. Could you unzip your jeans? You can _____ them _____ again.

Teacher's Notes:

Review phrasal verbs with students. Make sure students notice the structure of the

sentences, e.g.

You can (verb) it (preposition) again now.

Ask students to talk about the difference between:

1. Would you please remove your jacket?

2. Would you please take off your jacket?

Remove: formal term. may distance the patient from the health care worker

Take off: informal. puts patient and health care worker on the same level

Activity: Ask students to discuss the use of these instruments.

Before they start, review expressions like

It's used to…

It's used for…

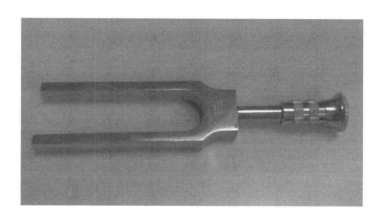

Role play. Unscramble the phrases the doctor uses to produce a dialogue between a doctor and a patient. Add the patient's responses. The doctor needs the patient to undress so s/he can examine him. The first one is done for you.

lift your skirt up over your tummy
pull down your underwear a bit
put your skirt down again
do up your shirt again
unbutton your shirt
pull your underwear up again
open your shirt

Ex 7:

Doctor: Could you please unbutton your shirt?

Patient: _____

Doctor: _____

Patient: _____

Doctor: _____

Patient: _____

Doctor: _____

Patient: _____

Doctor: _____

Patient: _____

Doctor: _____

Patient: _____

Doctor: _____

Patient: _____

Verbs of movement	
Asking a patient to move position	
Could you + verb	*Could you move up the bed?*
Would you + verb	*Would you stand up, please?*
I need you to + verb	*I need you to walk to the door.*
I'd like you to + verb…	*I'd like you to turn over now*

Ex 8: Match the descriptions 1 – 12   with the pictures a - l

1. turn your head to the side

2. lie on your back

3. bend your elbow

4. poke out your tongue

5. turn over on your tummy

6. raise your arm

7. roll onto your side

8. bend up your knee

9. bend your knee

10. bend over and try to touch your toes

11. look to the left

12. sit up

Day 4

1: Effective Patient Communication Skills III: Discussing Test Results and Treatment

2: Charts and Documentation

3: Preparing for OSCEs (or Equivalent Spoken Clinical Examinations) **part 1**

4: Developing Assessment Tools & Feedback Opportunities

1: Effective Patient Communication Skills III: Discussing Test Results and Treatment

Discussing test results

The language used to talk about test results:

- maths to talk about numerical values

- language to discuss increase in /decrease in

- scientific terms

Some examples of units in course books dealing with the language used to discuss test results

'Cambridge English for Nursing' Intermediate + Unit 5

with permission from the authors, Virginia Allum and Patricia McGarr

UNIT 5 Medical specimens

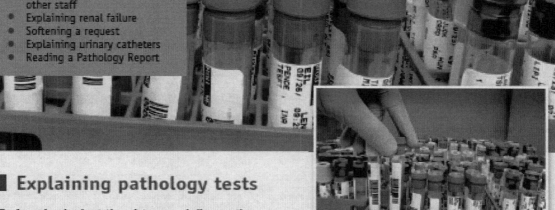

Aims
- Explaining pathology tests
- Asking for clarification
- Checking understanding
- Telephone skills: contacting other staff
- Explaining renal failure
- Softening a request
- Explaining urinary catheters
- Reading a Pathology Report

Explaining pathology tests

1 **a** In pairs, look at the picture and discuss the following questions.

   1 Are you familiar with the Pathology department in hospital?
   2 What kinds of tests are done there?
   3 Why is it important for nurses to understand the results of pathology tests?

b ▶5.1 Listen to a conversation between Mrs Faisal, a patient, and Frances, the Ward Nurse, and answer the following questions.

   1 What symptoms does Mrs Faisal have?
   2 What condition might she have?
   3 What is the name of the test which will be performed at Pathology?
   4 What does Frances have to collect from the patient?

Communication focus: asking for clarification

2 **a** In pairs, discuss the following questions.

- If you were unsure of an instruction or some information, how would you ask for clarification in English?
- Why is it important to clarify any instructions you don't understand?

b ▶5.1 Listen to the conversation again. Match the extracts (1–5) to the responses (a–e).

1 It burns when I go to the toilet, and I have to go all the time.	a Yes, the sample is less likely to have bacteria …
2 Is that right?	b Yes. It hurts when the urine comes out, …
3 What was it?	c Right. So what you're saying is that it hurts when you're actually passing urine …
4 He'll want you to do a urine specimen …	d Its full name is *urinary tract infection*.
5 Less contamination?	e OK. So you want me to do a urine specimen, do you?

c Complete the following clarification strategies using the words in the box.

intonation   repeat   paraphrase   clarify

1 _____ the information back to the speaker.
2 _____ what has been said.
3 Use a questioning _____ pattern.
4 Ask the speaker to _____ what they have said.

d In pairs, practise using the clarification strategies to respond to the following sentences.

- I've got a lot of problems when I go to the toilet.
- It burns when I go to the toilet.
- I have to go to the toilet all of the time.
- You might have a urinary tract infection.
- The doctor will want you to do a urine specimen.
- There's less contamination with a midstream specimen.

e In pairs, practise giving information and asking for clarification. Student A, you are Frances; Student B, you are Mrs Faisal. Remember to use the clarification strategies. Swap roles and practise again.

Share your knowledge

In small groups, discuss the following questions and then feed back your group's ideas to the class.

- How do you ensure privacy for your patients?
- What cultural issues are important in providing privacy?
- When might a patient request a chaperone?

Communication focus: checking understanding

3 **a** ▶ 5.2 Listen to the rest of the conversation between Mrs Faisal and Frances, and put the following extracts in the correct order.

☐ Try to catch the middle part of the urine stream.
☐ You need to clean the area around the urethra from front to back with these disposable wipes.
☐ Tighten the lid before you give me the specimen container, please.
☐ Don't touch the inside of the container when you take the lid off.
☐ Wash your hands thoroughly.

b ▶ 5.2 Frances uses several strategies to check understanding. Match the strategies (1–4) to the expressions from the dialogue (a–d). Listen again and check your answers.

1 Ask the patient to repeat the information back to you	a Could you repeat back the steps for me so I can be sure you followed my explanation?
2 Ask the patient to demonstrate the use of the equipment	b Do you understand/see what I mean?
3 Ask for clarification to ensure the patient understands what has been said	c Can you show me how you'll hold the specimen jar?
4 Ask the patient to list the steps of a procedure or process	d Right, so step one is?

Charting and documentation: Pathology Report

Pathology Reports are usually sent to the ward via the hospital intranet. A paper copy is also sent to the ward and filed in the patient's notes as a permanent record.

9 a In pairs, discuss the following questions.

1 Are you familiar with Pathology Reports?
2 What sort of information do they contain?
3 When do nurses refer to them?
4 Are you familiar with Pathology Reports online, i.e. on the hospital intranet?
5 When would a nurse phone a patient's doctor about a pathology result?

b In pairs, look at the Pathology Report on page 45 and answer the following questions.

1 What information does this Pathology Report contain?
2 What test was performed?
3 What type of specimen was collected?
4 What time was the specimen collected?
5 When was the specimen analysed in the lab?
6 What did the pathologist notice under the microscope?
7 What do you think *proteus mirabilis* is the name of?
8 What kind of drugs are ampicillin, cephalexin, trimethoprim and nitrofurantoin?
9 What comment did the pathologist make about Mrs Chu's specimen?

2: Charts and Documentation

Much of the writing in hospitals is formulaic

- charts e.g care pathways

- forms e.g lab request

- drug orders

- prescription charts

Other forms of writing may be:

- Writing short messages e. g phone messages

- Writing patient notes

- writing notes on a handover sheet

- writing referral letters

- keeping a reflective journal

- writing academic articles

The written language used will include:

- abbreviations (may be different depending on area)

- acronyms

- medical terminology

- everyday health terms

- reported speech - must be used to document what patient said (objective)

Collecting resources:

1. Hospital Charts

Excerpts from 'English for Medical Purposes: Spelling and Vocabulary'

Example of an Incident Report

This page to be completed by the Senior Staff Member on duty

6. Did the injured person stop work:

Yes ☐   No ☐   If yes, state date: Time:

Outcome:

☐ Treated by Doctor   ☐ Lodged Workers Comp Claim   ☐ Referred to RTW Coordinator

☐ OHS Authority notified   ☐ Returned to normal duties   ☐ Referred to OHS Coordinator &/or

☑ Hospitalised   ☐ Returned to alternative duties   OHS Committee

7. Incident or accident investigation

(Comments to include identified causal factors):

Name & Signature of Supervisor: Date:

8. Remedial actions:

☐ Conduct task analysis   ☐ Re-instruct persons involved   ☐ Improve design / construction / guarding

☐ Conduct hazard systems audit   ☐ Improve resident /staff skills mix   ☐ Add to inspection program

☐ Develop/ review tasks procedures   ☐ Provide debriefing and/or counselling   ☐ Improve communication / reporting procedures

☐ Improve work environment   ☐ Request maintenance   ☐ Improve security

☐ Review OH&S policy/programs   ☐ Improve personal protection   ☐ Temporarily relocate employees involved

☐ Replace equipment / tools   ☐ Improve work congestion/ housekeeping   ☐ Falls Prevention Assessment

☐ Improve work organization   ☐ Investigate safer alternatives   ☐ Request MSDS (Materials Safety Data Sheet)

☐ Develop and/or provide training   ☐ Other (specify)

What, in your own words, has been implemented or planned to prevent recurrence:

9. Remedial actions completed:

Signed (Supervisor):   Title: Date:

10. Review comments

H.R. Manager:

OHS Committee Meeting:

Reviewed by CEO / OHS Coordinator (Signed):   Date:

term	adjective	meaning
completion	completed by	paperwork which is filled in
(on) duty (duties)	dutiful	a work shift
lodgement of a claim	(to lodge a claim) lodged	send in a claim for compensation
coordinator	coordinated by	bring in all relevant people to help with something
notification	notified	let someone know about an incident
hospitalisation	hospitalised	keep a person in hospital for treatment
	alternative	different type of
investigation	investigative	look into the reasons for something
cause	causal	thing or things which made the incident occur
remedy	remedial	do something to make something better
analysis	analyse	check everything to find the cause or causes of the incident
hazard	hazardous	something which is dangerous
construction	constructed with	built using
audit	audited	review a procedure against a standard of care
debriefing (to debrief)	debriefed	talk about an incident afterwards so staff can express their feelings
relocation	relocated	put in a different place
replacement	replaced	exchanged with something new or better
training	trained by	specific workplace course
implementation	implemented by	put into action by

From: 'English for Medical Purposes: The Heart'

Integrated Care Pathways – Coronary Artery Angioplasty

What is an Integrated Care Pathway?

Integrated care pathways are task orientated care plans which detail essential steps in the care of patients with a specific clinical problem.

They may also be known as coordinated care pathways, care pathways, care maps or anticipated recovery pathways.

Care pathways differ from Nursing Care Plans which are based on a nursing assessment of a patient problem. Care plans have four components:

1. The nursing care problem and statement of the nursing approach to solve those problems

2. The expected outcome of the nursing care

3. The specific nursing actions to resolve the problem

4. Evaluation of the patient's response to nursing care and readjustment of that care as required

In contrast, Integrated Care Pathways are used for a specific clinical condition e.g Coronary Artery Angioplasty. They describe the tasks to be carried out when caring for a patient after a procedure as well as the timing and sequence of these tasks.

Ex 6 Look at the example below of a Care Pathway for

Coronary Angioplasty. Then, answer the following questions

1. What is the name of the patient?

2. When did he have the Coronary Angioplasty?

3. What is the date of the current Care Pathway?

CORONARY ANGIOPLASTY	Surname: Brown First Name: Bill Hospital Number: 145678 Ward : Blossom Bed no: 14			
Day 2 :	Date: 16/ 05/2010			
	Initial (performed) X (not performed) V (variance) N/A (Not Applicable	AM	PM	ND
Consultations / Referrals	Reviewed by Consultant			
Assessments / Investigations	Observations (T,P,R BP, Sa O $_2$) qds			
	Check radial site / groin site			
	Circulation Obs (C W M S)			
	Monitoring ceased			
	Pathology – FBC, CE			
	Notify significant ↑CE			
	Notify significant ↓platelets			
	ECG attended			
Comfort & Pain Management	Analgesia given as ordered			
Hygiene, Safety & Mobility	Care as per Falls Assessment Score _____			
	Ambulated gently			
	Hygiene attended with assistance / independently			
Hydration & Nutrition	Cardiac diet tolerated			
	Normal fluid intake tolerated			
Elimination	Fluid Balance ceased			
	Bowels charted			
Medication	Medications given as charted			
Wound Management & Treatments	IV removed			
	Sheath insertion site checked			
Skin Integrity	Care as per Nortons Score _____			
Education / Support	Discussed and reassured patient / family re procedure			
	Completed post Angioplasty Instruction Sheet			
Special Needs				
Discharge Planning	Patient's discharge needs re-assessed & actioned			
	Medication Profile completed			

Ex 7: Match the terms from the Care Pathway 1- 9 with their meanings a – i

1. V	a. electrocardiograph
2. N/A	b. Full Blood count
3. SaO$_2$	c. cardiac enzymes, after injury to the heart
4. qds	d. intravenous
5. C W M S	e. oxygen saturation
6. FBC	f. Not Applicable: action has not occurred
7. C E	g. Circulation Observations: Colour, Warmth, Movement, Sensation
8. ECG	h. four times a day
9. IV	i. variation: result not expected

Writing messages – Taking telephone messages

From 'Cambridge English for Nursing' Intermediate Plus, unit 10

with permission from authors Virginia Allum and Patricia McGarr

Telephone skills: referring a patient

2 **a** Ward staff often need to make telephone referrals to allied health departments or services. In pairs, look at the telephone referral form below and discuss the following questions.

1 Who referred Lidia to the District Nursing Service?
2 Where was she referred from?
3 Who is her next of kin?

TELEPHONE REFERRAL FORM

Service referred to	District Nursing Service
Name of patient	Lidia (1) ___Vassily___
Address	24 Spring Lane, Exeter
Entry to home (circle)	Digital Code /(Key) If by key, name of carer with spare key: (2) _____
Phone number	(3) _____
GP	Dr Serena (4) _____
Referred by	Andrea Dubois (RN)
Place of referral	Alexandra Hospital
Diagnosis	Stroke, mod. left-sided weakness, difficulty swallowing
Assistance with ADLs (circle)	(5) bathing mobility nutrition
Diet (circle)	(6) normal soft diabetic Other requirements (cultural/religious)
Delivery of meals (circle)	(7) Yes/No
Home assessment booked (circle)	(8) Yes/No If Yes, date booked: (9) _____
Aids / Equipment (circle if need to be ordered)	walking frame shower chair oxygen nebuliser
Next of kin	Larissa (daughter)
Phone number:	01265 781 992

b ▶ 10.2 Andrea, the Ward Nurse, rings Nadine, the District Nurse, to discuss Lidia's referral to the District Nursing Service. Listen to the conversation and complete the sections of the referral form marked 1–9.

c Speaking on the telephone to fluent speakers is often particularly difficult when under pressure. In pairs, discuss the following questions.

- Have you had difficulties with telephone communication?
- What type of situations have you found challenging?
- Which of the following strategies for effective telephone communication have you used?

Strategies for effective telephone communication

- Ask the fluent speaker to slow down as soon as you have difficulty understanding.

- Don't wait to ask the speaker to slow down until you are really lost.

- When you are taking down important details, repeat the information back so that you are sure you have understood.

- Do not be embarrassed to ask more than once if you are still not sure.

d ▶ 10.2 Listen to the telephone conversation again and tick the sentences you hear. You may hear both sentences in each pair.

1 a ☐ I'm sorry. What was your name again, please?
   b ☐ Sorry, what was your name?
2 a ☐ Could you please spell that for me?
   b ☐ Can you spell it?
3 a ☐ Can you say that again, please?
   b ☐ Could you please repeat that? I didn't catch the last numbers.
4 a ☐ Sorry, I didn't catch that.
   b ☐ Would you mind speaking a little slower, please? I'm having trouble following you.

e In pairs, practise making a referral for district nursing services. Student A, you are a Ward Nurse; Student B, you are a District Nurse. Use the referral form on page 79 and Mr Vogel's notes on page 91. Remember to use effective telephone strategies. Swap roles and practise again.

Transcript of the conversation

Nadine: District Nursing Service. Nadine Melesky speaking.

Andrea: Hello, it's Andrea here from 17 East at the Alexandra Hospital.

Nadine: I'm sorry. What was your name again, please?

Andrea: It's Andrea, Andrea Dubois from the Alexandra Hospital. I've got an 80-year-old lady I'd like to refer to you for some District Nursing services. Can I give you the details now?

Nadine: Wait a minute, let me get a referral form. OK, here it is. Yes, I'm ready, er, it was Andrea, wasn't it?

Andrea: That's right. Andrea Dubois from the Alexandra Hospital.

Nadine: Thanks, Andrea. Um, and what's the patient's name, please?

Andrea: I've got a Lidia Vassily for you.

Nadine: Oh, OK. Could you please spell that for me?

Andrea: Sure. It's L-I-D-I-A. She's Russian. And the surname's spelled V-A-double S-I-L-Y.

Nadine: Would you mind speaking a little slower, please? I'm having trouble following you.

Andrea: Yes, of course. It's hard over the phone, isn't it? Her family name is V-A S-S-I-L-Y.

Nadine: Vassily, right. Double S, one L. Got it, thanks.

Andrea: Her address is 24 Spring Lane, Exeter. It's a bungalow. The spare key's with her daughter, Larissa. Her daughter's also her next of kin.

Nadine: OK. Do you have Lidia's home phone number, please?

Andrea: Yes, I've got it here. It's oh one two six five, six four four, seven five three.

Nadine: Could you please repeat that? I didn't catch the last numbers.

Andrea: Yes, sure. Where is it? Here we are: oh one two six five, six four four, seven five three. Did you get that?

Nadine: Yes, thanks. Oh one two six five, er, six four four, seven five three. Is that correct?

Andrea: Yes, that's right. Do you want me to give you her daughter's number, too?

Nadine: Yes, please.

Andrea: Her daughter's name is Larissa and she's Lidia's next of kin, as I said. Her phone number is oh one two six five, seven eight one, nine nine two.

Nadine: Oh one two six five, seven eight one, nine nine two. Thanks.

Andrea: Lidia's GP is Dr Serena Hanif. I'll spell that for you. It's H-A-N-I-F.

Nadine: Serena Hanif. Yes, OK. H-A-N-I-F.

Andrea: Lidia had a stroke three weeks ago. She's got moderate left-sided weakness and still has some difficulty swallowing. She needs quite a lot of help with her ADLs, especially bathing and mobility. She's quite unsteady on her feet and uses a walking frame.

Nadine: Does she have a walking frame or will I have to order one?

Andrea: No, it's OK. She's already got a walking frame. She might need a shower chair, though. I think it'd be better to wait until after she has a home assessment done before any aids are ordered. The home assessment has been booked for 12th June.

Nadine: Er, home assessment 12th June. That's Monday, 12th June, right?

Andrea: Yes, that's it. Lidia's daughter asked if you could let her know what time the home assessment's being done so she can come over to her mother's house. She and her sister are a great support. Lidia's house will need some adaptions and her daughters want some advice on the sort of aids which are available to make things easier.

Nadine: OK. How's she managed with her diet?

Andrea: She's been managing a soft diet for a few days now.

Nadine: Mm, soft diet. Does she need her meals delivered to her at home?

Andrea: No. Her daughters are very supportive, and they'll help her with shopping and meal preparation. They know the sort of food she likes. No, forty mg not fifty …

Nadine: Sorry, I didn't catch that.

Andrea: Oh, no, I'm sorry, Nadine, someone just asked me a question. I got distracted. Er, I think I've given you all the information you need. Her discharge summary will be sent to you in the next day or so. Is there anything else you need to know?

Nadine: No, I think I've got everything. Er; thanks for being patient with me.

Andrea: No problem and thanks for your help.

Activity 10 In pairs, discuss

1. the areas which the nurse has difficulty

2. the strategies which would help students with taking messages on the phone?

Writing the patient record

Excerpt from 'Record keeping: Guidance for nurses and midwives'

from www.nmc-uk.org/

The way in which nurses and midwives keep records is usually set by their employer. The NMC recognises that, because of this, nurses and midwives may use different methods for keeping records. However, the principles of good record keeping are well established, and should reflect the core values of individuality and partnership working. Good record keeping is an integral part of nursing and midwifery practice, and is essential to the provision of safe and effective care. It is not an optional extra to be fitted in if circumstances allow. National programmes for the use of information communication technology and electronic record keeping are being introduced throughout the UK. Although electronic records are evolving, it is clear from nurses and midwives that paper based records are still commonly used. This guidance applies to both paper and electronic records. It explains what we expect from all nurses and midwives.

Good record keeping, whether at an individual, team or organisational level, has many important functions. These include a range of clinical, administrative and educational uses such as:

• helping to improve accountability

• showing how decisions related to patient care were made

• supporting the delivery of services

• supporting effective clinical judgements and decisions

• supporting patient care and communications

• making continuity of care easier

• providing documentary evidence of services delivered

• promoting better communication and sharing of information between members of the multi-professional healthcare team

• helping to identify risks, and enabling early detection of complications

• supporting clinical audit, research, allocation of resources and performance planning, and

• helping to address complaints or legal processes.

The Data Protection Act (1998) defines a health record as "consisting of information about the physical or mental health or condition of an identifiable individual made by or on behalf of a health professional in connection with the care of that individual." The principles of good record keeping apply to all types of records, regardless of how they are held. These can include:

• handwritten clinical notes

• emails

• letters to and from other health professionals

• laboratory reports

• x-rays

• printouts from monitoring equipment

• incident reports and statements

• photographs

• videos

• tape-recordings of telephone conversations

• text messages.

Principles of good record keeping

1. Handwriting should be legible.

2. All entries to records should be signed. In the case of written records, the person's name and job title should be printed alongside the first entry.

3. In line with local policy, you should put the date and time on all records. This should be in real time and chronological order and be as close to the actual time as possible.

4. Your records should be accurate and recorded in such a way that the meaning is clear.

5. Records should be factual and not include unnecessary abbreviations, jargon, meaningless phrases or irrelevant speculation.

6. You should use your professional judgement to decide what is relevant and what should be recorded.

7. You should record details of any assessments and reviews undertaken and provide clear evidence of the arrangements you have made for future and ongoing care. This should also include details of information given about care and treatment.

8. Records should identify any risks or problems that have arisen and show the action taken to deal with them.

9. You have a duty to communicate fully and effectively with your colleagues, ensuring that they have all the information they need about the people in your care.

10. You must not alter or destroy any records without being authorised to do so.

11. In the unlikely event that you need to alter your own or another healthcare professional's records, you must give your name and job title, and sign and date the

original documentation. You should make sure that the alterations you make, and the original record, are clear and auditable.

12. Where appropriate, the person in your care, or their carer, should be involved in the record keeping process.

13. The language that you use should be easily understood by the people in your care.

214. Records should be readable when photocopied or scanned.

15. You should not use coded expressions of sarcasm or humorous abbreviations to describe the people in your care.

16. You should not falsify records.

Confidentiality

17. You need to be fully aware of the legal requirements and guidance regarding confidentiality and ensure your practice is in line with national and local policies.

18. You should be aware of the rules governing confidentiality in respect of the supply and use of data for secondary purposes.

19. You should follow local policy and guidelines when using records for research purposes.

20. You should not discuss the people in your care in places where you might be overheard. Nor should you leave records, either on paper or on computer screens, where they might be seen by unauthorised staff or members of the public.

21. You should not take or keep photographs of any person, or their family, that are not clinically relevant.

Access

22. People in your care should be told that information on their health records may be seen by other people or agencies involved in their care.

23. People in your care have a right to ask to see their own health records. You should be aware of your local policy and be able to explain it to the person.

24. People in your care have the right to ask for their information to be withheld from you or other health professionals. You must respect that right unless withholding such information would cause serious harm to that person or others.

25. If you have any problems relating to access or record keeping, such as missing records or problems accessing records, and you cannot sort out the problem yourself, you should report the matter to someone in authority. You should keep a record that you have done so.

26. You should not access the records of any person, or their family, to find out personal information that is not relevant to their care.

Disclosure

27. Information that can identify a person in your care must not be used or disclosed for purposes other than healthcare without the individual's explicit consent. However, you can release this information if the law requires it, or where there is a wider public interest.

28. Under common law, you are allowed to disclose information if it will help to prevent, detect, investigate or punish serious crime or if it will prevent abuse or serious harm to others.

Information systems

29. You should be aware of, and know how to use, the information systems and tools that are available to you in your practice.

330. Smartcards or passwords to access information systems must not be shared. Similarly, do not leave systems open to access when you have finished using them.

31. You should take reasonable measures to check that your organisation's systems for

recording and storing information, whether by computer, email, fax or any other electronic means, are secure. You should ensure you use the system appropriately, particularly in relation to confidentiality.

Personal and professional knowledge and skills

32. You have a duty to keep up to date with, and adhere to, relevant legislation, case law and national and local policies relating to information and record keeping.

33. You should be aware of, and develop, your ability to communicate effectively within teams. The way you record information and communicate is crucial. Other people will rely on your records at key communication points, especially during handover, referral and in shared care.

34. By auditing records and acting on the results, you can assess the standard of the record keeping and communications. This will allow you to identify any areas where improvements might be made.

Further reading

This guidance is supported by further notes and frequently asked questions which are available at www.nmc-uk.org

European Convention on Human Rights Act 1950

National Health Service Venereal Disease Regulations (SI 1974 No 29)

Access to Health Records (1990)

The Computer Misuse Act 1990

Human Fertilisation and Embryology Act 1990

The Civil Evidence Act (1995)

Caldicott Report (DH) 1997

Access to Medical Reports Act (1998)

Data Protection Act (1998)

The Road Traffic Act 1998

The Data Protection Order (2000)

The Electronic Communications Act (2000)

The Freedom of Information Act 2000

The Terrorism Act 2000

The Freedom of Information (Scotland) Act 2002

The Communications Act 2003

Confidentiality: NHS Code of Practice (2006)

Security Management NHS Code of Practice (2007)

NHS Information Governance Guidance on legal and professional obligations (2007)

3. Preparing for OSCEs (or Equivalent Spoken Clinical Examinations) part 1

What are OSCEs?

OSCEs or Objective Structured Clinical Examination is a type of examination which is used in health sciences e.g. medicine and nursing. It tests clinical skills as well as communication. OSCEs are usually organised around a circuit of short activities. Each part of the activity takes around 5–10 minutes. Students undertake a simulation of a scenario where they practise on a patient (a real patient or an actor).

Example of an OSCA in the Diploma of Nursing –administration of a sublingual medication

Did the student perform the following skills:	Yes	No
Introduces self to the client	☐	☐
Determines client's identification	☐	☐
Accesses relevant documentation	☐	☐
Explains interventions/procedures using appropriate communication skills	☐	☐
Obtains consent for the procedure	☐	☐
Cleans hands as necessary	☐	☐
Demonstrates use of MIMs	☐	☐
Checks 5 rights: Right route, right medication, right date/time, right person, right dose	☐	☐
Checks allergy status	☐	☐
Ensures privacy	☐	☐
Assists client to gain a appropriate position to receive medication		
Administers appropriate medication correctly as per medication chart and scope of job role	☐	☐
Assesses client's response to interventions	☐	☐
Ensures client comfort	☐	☐
Document the results	☐	☐
Reports changes in client health or condition to the supervisor & documents in progress notes	☐	☐

Evaluates own performance	☐	☐
Complies with Occupational Health & Safety Guidelines throughout every contact and all interventions	☐	☐
Complies with infection control guidelines throughout every contact and all interventions	☐	☐
Performed skills and documentation in a timely manner	☐	☐

Activity11: In pairs, discuss the following questions

1. Using the above OSCE as an example, write a list of the functional language needed to perform the elements of the OSCE. For example, 'Introduces self to the client' – introduce yourself to a patient using appropriate title.

2. How can teachers adapt OSCEs as role plays?

3. Is it necessary for EMP language teachers to know about the technical aspects of the OSCE e.g 'Checks 5 rights'?

4. What other language practice can OSCEs test?

1: Academic Writing and Abstracts

NURS 460: Nursing Research

University of Kansas School of Nursing

http://www2.kumc.edu/instruction/nursing/nurs460smith/overview.html

Good resources for Nursing Research

Activity 12: Read the article below and design an activity which helps students understand the terms which relate to research.

Reading Nursing Research to Critique a Study and to Summarize Findings for Use in Practice

http://www2.kumc.edu/instruction/nursing/nurs460smith/460critiquingreseach.html

Research must be used to develop the discipline and science of nursing. Learning how to critically read **nursing research** then is crucial in its application to practice. First, a review of some of the common research language and definitions of the sections seen in **quantitative research** articles are covered. As you go through the chapter, you will learn how to **critically read** each section of the research article. You are given many examples to help you get the most information from comparing what you have read to colleagues' reviews of articles on the same topic. You will learn some questions to pose about the quality of the research as well as the appropriateness of using the findings in your own practice.

Nurses must learn how to read, understand, and **critique** research articles (Zanotti, 2000). Reading about nursing research should get you in the habit of posing questions about the quality of the research and about the appropriateness of using the research results in your own practice (Snyder-Halpern, 1991). As you go through this assignment, you will learn how to critically read each section of the research article. You are given many examples to help you get the most information from comparing what you have read to colleagues' reviews of articles on the same topic. When using research findings in practice, it is best to find replication of results in several studies before using the research in your practice (Linquist, Brauer, Lekander, & Foster, 1990). After reading and **summarizing** the research literature, on a topic the nurse then develops a detailed plan for utilization of selected research findings in her practice. This plan included specific actions for communication of the research findings to other nurses and physicians, and a method of evaluation to be used after the research was put into practice. Thus, the examples given here are from reading several articles on the same research topic.

Reading Research Articles

This overview is an example illustrating how to read research articles. First, ascertain the problem being examined by reading the title and abstract to get a summary of the study. The introductory paragraphs of the article must clearly state the significance of the problem described in previous studies on this topic in the literature. Then, determine if the research design and methods used are appropriate for the problem under study. Next, the reader reads the **data collection procedures** described in the design and the **data** that were analyzed. The reader determines if appropriate statistical tests have been applied to the data collected in the particular study. There are typically graphs and tables that are visual interpretations of the data. These visuals should give you an understanding of measures of central tendency, such as the **mean** and **standard deviation**, and **data distribution**. The normal curve and measures of central tendency are essential to display. The process of inferring from a **sample** to a clinical situation in terms of conclusions should be discussed. Review the authors' discussion comments and rate them as acceptable and important for clinical practice and as contributing to the subject matter. You must, however, read all of the sections and determine if the authors' implications for practice are correct from the data they obtained. Examples in the Tables will help you critique the sections of the article.

Questions to Use When Reviewing Research Articles

To guide your critique of a research article, use the following questions when reading each section of a quantitative study. Reading an article while thinking about these questions, which are related to quality of the study, is important for determining if you should put the research into practice. Use the list of questions in Table 1 to help you understand the process of reading each section of the research article.

These examples are the author's summary from reading five interdisciplinary, quantitative research articles on the same topic of congestive heart failure (CHF). The overall research objectives of these studies were to determine what factors relate to older persons with congestive heart failure (CHF) having to be readmitted to the hospital (Heidenreich, Ruggerio, & Massie, 1999; Rich, Beckham, Wittenberg, & Freedland, 1995; Shah, Der, Ruggerio, Heidenreich, & Massie, 1998; Smith, 1991).

Title and Abstract of the Article

Does the **title** indicate the research is important for nursing?

Does the **abstract** include information from each section of the article?

For example, all five studies had clear title and abstract statements. Information on the problem, **theory** and literature synthesis, **research design** and **statistical analyses**; and major findings are listed. However, the research questions or **hypothesis** were missing from 3 of the abstracts. Another common issue in reading abstracts is to distinguish the specific problem identified for the research, and how the actual data that is collected represents or matches the problem.

Statement of the Problem

Is the problem identified early and stated clearly and concisely?

Is the problem stated in terms, which are specific and narrow enough to study?

Is the problem important or significant for nursing practice?

For example, the descriptive studies provided evidence that re-admissions to hospitals of patients with congestive heart failure (CHF) were very frequent and thus, a very costly problem. The experimental studies state the problem as a need for teaching or follow-up home care by nursing, which can reduce readmission costs. Unfortunately, a limitation of the studies was that no cost data were collected.

Review of Literature and Theoretical or Conceptual Framework

Is the study problem described within the context of existing knowledge and previous research on the topic and has interdisciplinary literature been investigated?

Does the **review of the literature** provide supporting evidence to show the need for carrying out the research?

Is consultation with experts in the field apparent?

Are documentation and selection of **references** appropriate?

For example, the literature review for these studies all referenced recent interdisciplinary studies done on patient teaching for CHF. Explain how the literature review or theory was applied to this study. For example, 3 of the 5 studies used the cost effectiveness theory and one used adult learning theory. These theories were used to guide selection of **questionnaires** and outcome data. Theories were used to limit the research population to CHF patients who had repeated Emergency Room visits and re-hospitalizations. There should be discussion of a **conceptual framework** or **theory** appropriate to use for guiding the study. Two of the five studies had no theory or conceptual framework, and therefore were not specific in the questionnaires used or data gathered. Results from that study were too broad to be helpful for nursing practice. Unfortunately, a limitation was that only one of the authors had gerontology as a specialty area. Thus, the other research may not have the benefit of interventions tested, which were developed with older adults in mind.

Research Design

Is the design appropriate to answer the questions indicated by the problem?

Are correct statistics used to test the study hypotheses?

Were the measures of central tendency and descriptive/summary **statistics** before further analysis of data?

What do the terms clinical significance versus statistical significance mean?

How many **survey responses** do you need to demonstrate feasibility, and what is this measure of feasibility (e.g., if 50% of respondents say the message is interesting, is that enough, or do you need 80%?

What happens if the researchers don't get enough responses?

For example, of the 5 studies reviewed, 3 were **descriptive research** design, and 2 were **correlation research** design. For example, the descriptive studies were explanatory; therefore, the age, education level, and severity of disease could be described along with the number of ER visits and returns to the hospital. The correlational designs were used to look for associations; therefore, the number of ER visits of CHF patients following hospital discharge could be compared to the number of nurse follow-up telephone calls and videotapes on home CHF care given to the family.

A portion of the research design review should explain how the research variables and the hypothesized relationships were selected (e.g., severity of illness of the patients in relation to the teaching methodology needed at discharge by the family). There should be links between variables in the conceptual framework and those measured in the data collection.

Note any probable sources of error that might influence the results; for example, the ordinal data was not the correct type to collect for the tests used in the correlational studies. There were strengths and weaknesses in the statistics that were used; for example, all studies had been conducted in hospitals with elderly patients being treated for CHF; none were conducted in patients' homes where the researchers could observe day-by-day barriers to home CHF management.

As the joke below illustrates, when using statistics, assumptions about the appropriate statistic to analyze the data, cannot depend on miracles!

Results or Findings

Are the findings of this study relevant to your clinical practice?

Is there enough **evidence base** (data) to indicate this patient's problem can be minimized by using the nursing interventions tested in the study?

For example, to determine the extent to which these findings currently are being used in practice. You can interview faculty and nurse graduates and examine relevant textbooks.

Both experimental studies had evidence that indicated nurses telephoning or providing videotape patient education guidance decreased ER visits compared to control group patient samples.

The implications for nursing across all studies were that our profession needed to think in terms of populations of patients and what specific nursing interventions can contribute to improved outcomes including lower costs by decreasing hospital use. Then, you must decide on the application of the results to your own clinical practice (Kirchhoff, & Titler, 1994).

Journal Clubs for Research Reading

You may read research for clinical implications in journal clubs or workgroups of students, nurses, doctors, and even patients. You might facilitate a discussion around aspects of research on families managing complex home care, the research topic called care giving. There are a vast number of quantitative articles on this topic (Dracup, & Breu, 1978). Thus, one of the first discussion questions of your group might be, "What are problems that family care givers face when they are managing critically ill children, frail elders, or their terminal ill loved ones in their home?" Another discussion question might be, "What are the likely research designs to be used in describing these types of care giving problems, or are there nursing interventions for caregivers that have been tested in experimental research?" Your group would decide what the benefit of either type of article would be for the groups reading once the various articles were read (one article by each person). Next, each person shares the review of their article.

A further question for discussion would be: "Did the research article operationally define a family caregiver" or "what problem statement identified the variables to study?" "Did the researchers determine what care givers face when working with medical equipment needed in the home?" By the end of these workgroups research discussions, you will have a good overview of the research in the problem area you selected to read. You will also be able to learn from the opinions of the others in the group as well. This table has an example workgroup where each person shared their critique of a separate article on the topic of interest to nurse administrators.

Reading Research Articles for Using Research In Practice

Next, your critique should discuss "research utilization," a word used to describe the process of reading research critically to determine if there is enough scientific results of nursing research to put into practice (Butts, 1982; Fawcett, 1982; Sheridan, 1983; and Stetler, 1983, 1984). Research Utilization is "a process directed toward transfer of specific research-based knowledge into practice through the systematic use of a series of activities" (Dunn, 1983; Krueger, 1978). Activities for using research include: transformation of implications for practice from the research articles into what is known as a data based or evidence based clinical care plan (Horsley, Crane, Crabtree, & Wood 1983). Each care plan focuses on a researched problem and related nursing actions; and each uses the actual studies read to develop step-by-step instructions on how to introduce the new research based plan on a clinical unit (Barnard, 2000; King, Barnard, & Hoehn, 1981).

In other words, research can provide material for a new procedure or policy to support the need for change of services. In contrast, a nurse can use new research to improve her understanding of various situations (Stetler, & Marram, 1976; Stetler, 1983). The classic example is nurses implementing a structured preoperative teaching program that became standards that improved all surgical care (a 1971 study by Lindeman and Van Aernam). The discussion group readers can adapt the findings of the care giving studies to develop a care plan that they tested now being used for including family. Remember to keep reading, asking critical questions, and using appropriate quantitative research in your nursing practice. Then, you will truly have defined nursing practice as "merging science with compassion."

Additional Activities:

Activity 13. Talking about the pulse rate

You need:

- a watch or mobile phone with a second hand

- a handout sheet for students

Before you start, teach students how to take a radial pulse.

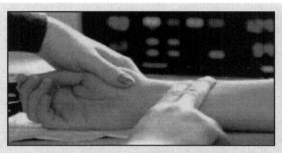

The Radial pulse is most commonly used to assess heart rate because it is the easiest to access. The radial artery is on the patient's inside forearm on the same side as the thumb.

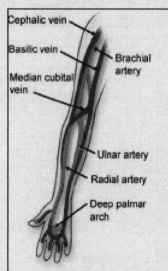

How to take a pulse

Equipment : a watch with a second hand (to count the number of beats over 60 seconds)

The pulse rate is written as
    <u>Number</u> beats per minute.

Lightly place the tips of your second and third fingers over the **radial** artery (located on the wrist). Do not use your thumb as the thumb has its own pulse. Count the number of beats for 60 seconds. As you become more confident you can count the number of beats for 30 seconds then double your answer.

<u>**The Pulse (cloze) . Choose words from the box below to fill in the spaces.**</u>

When taking a patient's pulse, the nurse is careful to note r_____ and c_____ . The normal pulse rate for an adult is between 60 and 80 _____ per minute. _____ refers to a fast pulse rate ,over 100 beats per minute. A _____ pulse rate ,under 60 beats a minute, is called bradycardia. It is also important to take note of the character of the pulse. In other words, what is the pulse like? Check the _____ of the pulse, that is, whether the pulse is regular or irregular. Finally, describe the strength or _____ of the pulse. A weak pulse is described as _____ ,while a strong force is described as _____ .

rate	tachycardia	rhythm	thready	slow
force	character	full	beats	

Aim: Students use appropriate language to

- ask for a patient's consent before a procedure

- describe a pulse

- talk about numbers

- describe the change in pulse rate after 5 mins of exercise.

Method: In pairs, Student A is the nurse/doctor and Student B is the patient.

Students write a short dialogue which includes:

- nurse/doctor asking for consent before taking the pulse

- taking a resting pulse (feel pulse at the wrist and count for one minute. Note that normal resting pulse is around 72 and regular, however athletes often have a regular pulse of below 60. This is OK)

- Make a note of the pulse and then ask the patient to run up and down stairs or run around for 5 mins.

- Take the pulse again. Record the pulse

- Report to the class what happened to the pulse rate after exercise.

Evaluation: What are examples of the language used?

Was this language expected?

Activity 14: In pairs, look at the picture and think of as many words as you can which are related to the picture. Feed back to the class explaining the use of the equipment.

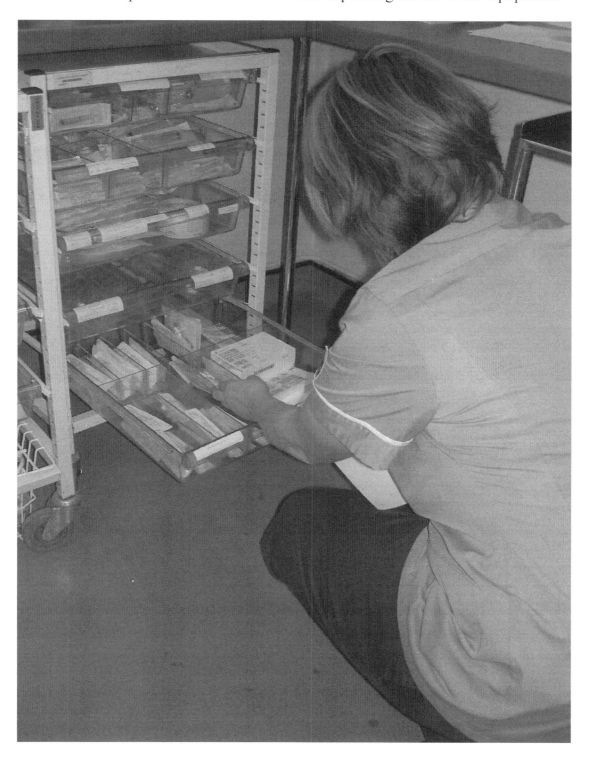

23020563R00125

Made in the USA
Middletown, DE
14 August 2015